RAGE FOR ORDER

Essays in Criticism

BY

AUSTIN WARREN

E 70

Ann Arbor Paperbacks

THE UNIVERSITY OF MICHIGAN PRESS

TO ELEANOR
and
FOR HOWARD

First edition as an Ann Arbor Paperback 1959
Copyright © 1948 by The University of Michigan
All rights reserved
Second printing 1962
Published in the United States of America by
The University of Michigan Press and simultaneously
in Toronto, Canada, by Ambassador Books Limited
Manufactured in the United States of America

PREFACE

THE title of this book couples together two contraries necessary to poetry or literature—intensity and calm; initial violence, sought and achieved discipline, which is not suppression but controlled and formal speech. Art can fail by opposite modes: by flatness and glibness, when the writer has no experience to master and to name but only a job of verbalizing; by obscurity and hysteria, when the writer is inadequate or has given up too soon. It succeeds when there is an equilibrium which is also a tension, when there is a rage waiting to be ordered and a rage to find, or to make, that ordering.

Poetry is a double, a triple, discipline. There is a technical, most specifically a linguistic, training, partly traditional but chiefly self-acquired, a deformation and reorganization of the language. There is also a spiritual discipline—of confronting disorder in one's self and in the world; of facing existentially, as a total human being living in time, the responsibility of vision and choice. The third discipline, one might say, is to unite the spiritual revolution and reconstitution to the linguistic or literary. But this is not a third stage. With a writer, the linguistic renaming or renovation and the self-searching and cosmos-confronting go on concurrently or in rapid alternation and reciprocity.

The poet's passionate desire to perceive order for himself (not to accept it as a stereotype, 'given,' handed down) makes his final creation a kind of world or cosmos; a concretely languaged, synoptically felt world; an ikon or image of the 'real world.' This view cannot be abstracted from the language and the mythic structure in which it is incarnated. To the extent that they would 'understand,' the reader and the critic must themselves repeat the double discipline; but the sequence is ordinarily to be reversed: the reader starts from the linguistic work of art, at which the poet's spiritual experience has ended.

The critic has his own rage for order, a passionate desire to discover, by analysis and comparison, the systematic vision of the world which is the poet's construction, his equivalent of a philosophical or other conceptual system. He judges it a test of a mode of order that it be imaginable as well as conceivable. He hypothesizes that the cosmos of a serious poet is, intuitively and dramatically, coherent. He seeks to define the spiritual cosmos of each and the specifically literary structure which corresponds to it. These are the enterprises of 'practical criticism,' of essays devoted to particular authors or literary works. But there is no practice without an implied theory, a theory under construction. It is scarcely possible for literary criticism to eschew participation in the deep need and search of our time, for general principles of order; it is certainly impossible to write, as poet or critic, without the search for an adequate poetics—an adequate theory of the nature and function of imaginative literature.

The earliest of the essays here assembled was written in 1936. Except for that on Hawthorne, they were first published in various quarterly reviews—the *American*, the *Southern*, the *Kenyon*, and the *Sewanee;* but they have been revised, chiefly by excision, for this book. In this process they profited from the counsel of Mr. George Dillon and Miss Genevieve White.

In our vast country, writers are often forced to live in isolation from their kind and to write for no perceptible group of readers. It gives one definable responsibility, relief, and comfort to have a place in which he can habitually and by invitation publish and to have that 'place' in a review with an editorial policy and an audience of corresponding coherence. I owe much to the editors who prompted these essays.

A second debt of which I am gratefully conscious is to the School of Letters at the University of Iowa, for some time a real intellectual community, and to my fellow-members.

Grateful acknowledgment is made to Alfred A. Knopf for permission to use the last five lines of the poem "The Idea of Order at Key West," from *Ideas of Order* by Wallace Stevens, New York, 1936.

February 18, 1947

CONTENTS

I

EDWARD TAYLOR

TO CRITICS of poetry, 'metaphysical' has become a term almost as troublesome as 'romantic.' Once pejorative, it has turned into an adjective of eulogy; but, as before, its scope remains uncertain. Sometimes it appears as a historical term, restricted to a literary movement which became obsolescent about 1650; sometimes it serves as a critical concept in the differentiation of one poetic 'kind' from another. With some critics, metaphysical poetry seems to be synonymous with Donne's, and specifically with Donne's *Songs and Sonnets,* and, in effect, with three or four of them: sometimes it appears a normative definition derived from the concluding stanzas of "Valediction Forbidding Mourning"; with other critics, it means all seventeenth-century poetry—presumably, that is, before 1660. With some, it means poetry with a discursive or public structure; with others, it includes as well *symboliste* poetry in which the narrative or logical continuum is chiefly absent and the movement from image to image effected by private association.

The term has manifest advantages over such former captions as 'Cavalier,' since (with both Johnson and Eliot) it belongs to literary history and criticism rather than to political history; but it should probably be abandoned for terms and concepts more precise or defined afresh for each use. For persons who deal in continuities, it is more profitable (since 'movements' ordinarily move at the impetus of a poetic 'first mover') to speak of the 'tradition' of Donne, or Pope, or Eliot, if they can remember that two or more 'traditions' may meet in the work of a particular poet; for characterization of poets historically near and sharing in some large and general traits we need such a term as 'baroque'; finally, and obviously, the work of each poet must be defined in terms of itself, as a unique work.

'Baroque' shall name such English poetry and prose antedating the neoclassical movement as would, by neoclassical standards, be judged 'false wit.' It subsumes the poetry of Quarles, Benlowes, Cleveland, Crashaw, and Donne; the prose of Andrewes, Browne, and Burton. Its philosophy is Christian and supernaturalist and incarnational, a philosophy admissive of miracle and hence of surprise; its aesthetic, by appropriate consequence, indorses bold figures, verbal and imaginal—such figures as the pun, the oxymoron, the paradox, the metaphor which links events from seemingly alien, discontinuous spheres. It likes polar mixtures—the shepherds and the magi, the colloquial and the erudite. If it provides ecstasies, it allows also of ingenuities: anagrams and acrostics and poems shaped like obelisks or Easter wings.

The baroque, in the visual arts and architecture, first identifies itself with the Catholic Counter Reformation; and, in poetry as well, a fully supernatural and sacramental conception of the world, a view which holds that miracles still occur in history, is the philosophy which best validates it. But such a view, if most completely represented by the doctrine and ethos of the Roman church, is approximately held by High Anglicans and is not absent from—but only re-

stricted by—Puritanism and Nonconformity: a supernaturalist treatment of biblical and apostolic history is common
to all seventeenth-century Christians.

'Metaphysical poetry,' taken to mean the poetry of Donne,
Carew, and Lord Herbert of Cherbury, is obviously an aristocratic poetry; and the older designation of 'Cavalier' poets
evokes the conception of courtly wits writing for the court.
But certain baroque English poets, Herbert and Quarles, won
Puritan acceptance, and not alone that of the Puritan gentry:
Pope dubs Quarles the "plebeians' darling." And a poetic
'epic' widely acceptable to Puritans, aristocrats and bourgeois
alike, was *The Divine Weeks,* Joshua Sylvester's 1605 translation from the French of a Huguenot nobleman, Guillaume
de Saluste du Bartas.

Milton was reared on Du Bartas. The curious conceit in
the "Nativity Ode," written while he was still enamored of
the "late fantastics," might have come from the fertile pages
of *The Divine Weeks:*

> So when the Sun in bed
> Curtain'd with cloudy red
>> Pillows his chin upon an Orient wave.....

Du Bartas assigns ever procreating Nature to a star-canopied
bedstead:

> Having therefore the Worlds wide curtain spread
> About the circuit of the fruitful Bed
> Where (to fill allwith her unnumbered kin)
> Kind Nature's self each moment lieth-in;
> To make the same forever admirable
> More stately-pleasant and more profitable,
> God th' Azure-Tester trimm'd with golden marks
> And richly spangled with bright glittering sparks.

[3]

His characteristic analogies compare not the less to the greater but the greater to the less, domesticating the wild or grand things into familiar properties of chamber, hearth, and barnyard. But the trait which most obviously differentiates his conceits from those of Donne is their externality: Donne is a psychologist and casuist whose remembered conceits are poetic correlatives for inner states. Du Bartas' conceits couple disjunct worlds—heaven and earth, animate and inanimate; but they do so only superficially, for his heaven is as material and external as his earth, and the images conjoined lie within a single dimension. Fancy, operating upon matter supplied by the memory, has matched counter with counter. The miracle is, at maximum, some Mosaic legerdemain of turning water into blood or turning water into dry land; it is never the Word becoming flesh.

With the Restoration of the Stuarts, England moved into a new literary era, of which—according to received genealogy —Jonson was the ancestral representative, Waller and Denham the approximate inaugurators, and Dryden the heroic figure. But the same Restoration effected an isolation of the New England colonies. Politically, theologically, and morally out of sympathy with the age which followed the collapse of their hopes for England, the colonists of Massachusetts Bay took little interest in the literature which was its product. If, for English literary history, the seventeenth century breaks, at about 1660, into contrasting periods, baroque and neoclassical, for American literary history the century constitutes a unit; and the advent of the new mode is delayed until the age of Anne—and that of Pope's correspondent and Boston's laureate, Mather Byles.

In spite of her contemporary celebration as a "Du Bartas

girl," Anne Bradstreet's long 'moralities' have nothing in common with the *Weeks* except their run-on couplets and their panoramic scope. But the humbler baroque ingenuities the New Englanders could reproduce. The anagram, with its cognate forms, which Dryden and Addison were to satirize, was a favorite genre for clerical wits. Attributing skill at it to Wilson, first pastor of the Boston church, Cotton Mather likens to creation *ex nihilo* this construction of

> anagrams, in which he made to start
> Out of mere nothings, by creating art
> Whole words of counsel; did to motes unfold
> Names, till they lessons gave richer than gold.....

Equally useful for edification was the pun.

New England wit is most readily illustrated out of elegies. The chief occasion when the arts serve piety was the death of some friend, relative, or eminent person. Then a funeral discourse was appropriate; the slatecarver's craft was summoned to incise skulls, skeletons, and cherubs; and funeral verse was requisite not only for addition to the memorial slate but, at more ambitious length, for use on a black-bordered broadside.

Despite the youthful Franklin's satire, the New England elegy, as written by its experts, was rarely dull. Nothing in the life of a 'saint' could be unordained by Providence; and one's name—in its sober normality or anagrammatically rearranged—or one's profession, or the disease one fatally suffered from were all motifs emblematic and apt for adaptation. No New England poet possessed the fertility of Cleveland, or of Dryden, whose "Elegy on Lord Hastings" turns to such brilliant account the smallpox from which the noble sufferer perished; but nothing debarred them from competition in kind. Thus the Revd. Nicholas Noyes, elegizing his friend, the Revd. Joseph Green, the "green and growing olive tree," devises all proper ethical verdancies; thus the Revd. Mr. Capen extendedly analogizes John Foster, deceased printer, to an old almanac which heaven shall revise and to which, revised, God will add his imprimatur. A more sophisticatedly playful performance, Benjamin Tompson's elegy for Woodmansey, Master of the Boston Latin School, pursues its fancy consistently: in *The Grammarian's Funeral,* the mourners are not towns, rivers, saints, or poets, but the eight parts of speech, the old schoolmaster's companions and servants.

> The Clouds of Tears did overcast their faces,
> Yea all were in most lamentable *Cases,*
> The five *Declensions* did the Work decline,
> And told the *Pronoun Tu,* the work is thine:
> But in this case those have no call to go
> That want the Vocative, and can't say O!
> Great honor was confer'd on *Conjugations,*
> They were to follow next to the *Relations.*
> *Amo* did love him best, and *Doceo* might
> Allege he was his Glory and Delight.
> But *Lego* said By me he got his skill,
> And therefore next the *Herse* I follow will ....
> A doleful day for *Verbs,* they look so *moody*
> They drove Spectators to a Mournful Study.....

Tompson, the "Renowned Poet of New England" (as his gravestone celebrated him) wrote no other elegy so sustained in mode as this intellectual divertissement, but he occasionally writes a witty stanza.

> The Vesper of his life's a constant Cry
> When will deaths curious claws these knots untie?

A crazie cage of bones curtained with Skin,
A Ruind Castle where great strength had beene.

That is a jagged and uneven series of which the second and third lines could scarcely have been written out of the seventeenth century.

Uneven too is the poetry of Edward Taylor (1645–1729), published for the first time in 1939 under the editorship of Thomas H. Johnson. Taylor, who migrated from Warwickshire to Massachusetts in 1668 and graduated from Harvard in 1671, must be accounted not only the least negligible American poet before Bryant but the latest of known poets writing in the English baroque.

Taylor has his minor ingenuities—for example, his tributes to Harvard's late president: in a quadruple acrostic, the 'trible' is an anagram, "Charles Chauncy—Call in the Churches," while the left-hand initials spell out "President Dyed"; an acrostic chronogram spells out the date of Chauncy's death and his age. Most elaborate in this kind is Taylor's verse letter to his prospective wife, an alphabetic acrostic containing a triangle which in turn encloses a circle. The triangle spells out:

> The ring of love my pleasant heart must bee
> Truly confined within the Trinitie,

and such, by the equivalence of Triangle and Trinity, the ring is; while the circle translates into:

> Loves Ring I send
> That hath no End.

These instances of what the century called "shaped verses" are simple extensions of the 'emblem,' the visualization of a metaphor.

In all his poetry Taylor is a wit. Like Andrewes and Crashaw, he puns in work of serious intentions. He can write: "This cur that is so curst"; Christ "died upon the cross to cross out sins." Nor is he unfamiliar with the more recondite oxymoron, the "dying life and living death," to be met with in Quarles and the Fletchers.

But his chief instrument is the conceit: the homely conceit. The imaginative distance between its terms is the distance between philosophical theology and anthropomorphic piety, and again between anthropomorphic piety and animism. It is not the hyperbolic or honorific use but the domesticating: the shock comes from the modernization, the provincializing, of the Infinite. Taylor's figures for the spiritual life, his constant matter, come from brewery or wine cellar; or from the stalls in the market place at Coventry; or from weaving, the familiar craft of his native Warwickshire; or from the traffic of sedans and coaches; or from the games played, in his youth, by the ungodly:

> Mine Heart's a Park or Chase of Sins: Mine Head
> 'S a Bowling Alley: sins play Ninehole here.
> Phansy's a Green: Sin Barly-breaks in't led.
> Judgment's a pingle: Blindeman's Buff's plaid there.

Taylor's most ambitious piece, *God's Determinations,* opens with a 'preface' in which, like Sylvester and Benlowes, Taylor, reversing the romantic procedure, analogizes nature to the crafts.

> Who Lac'de and Fillitted the earth so fine,
> With Rivers like green Ribbons Smaragdine?
> Who made the Sea's its Selvedge, and it locks
> Like a Quilt Ball within a Silver Box?
> Who Spread its Canopy? Or Curtains Spun?
> Who in this Bowling Alley bowld the Sun?

The obvious comment to make on this kind of writing is that, granted a certain auctorial inventiveness and charmed persistence, it could go on, like Whitman's naturalistic catalogues, without any reason for stopping. Beyond that, one sees that, within the general mode of 'nature = the artificed,' the poet feels no responsibility to arrange his tropes: they go outdoors, indoors, into my lady's chamber, into her wardrobe, without planned movement of parallelism or contrast. And from this absence of more than most general pattern, one sees the poet is scarcely conscious of his pattern's implications. What they are is clear. God, in creating the earth, did not operate like an architect whose responsibility limited itself to blueprints or like a Newtonian Engineer calculating masses and thrusts and pressures; he worked out his designs with the same manual detail with which a dressmaker puts together a dress or a carpenter makes a box. But the poet seems unaware how far his aesthetic refers back to his theology and, so, uncertain of what he is trying, in words, to do.

This 'preface' is not unfairly characteristic of what follows, a long poem partly in the set dialogue of the moralities, partly in lyric strophes. Its modest but indubitable success is in its logic, still more in its psychology. Taylor—even after reference to *Ductor Dubitantium* and *Treatise on the Religious Affections*—is a respectable, a sensitive, casuist.

After a preluding dialogue between Justice and Mercy, Taylor briefly represents the rebellion, from Satan's army, of the elect; and then the drama—an inner drama—begins. Satan is furious at the defection from his ranks and begins a series of dialectic onslaughts calculated to weaken the morale of the recusants. The converts are divided into three 'ranks' or categories; and Satan addresses himself in turn, with psychiatric shrewdness, to the situation of each. As in Herbert's "The Collar," the subtle argumentation is entirely directed against the reality of the religious experience. It is precarious to represent God as a dialectician; and Taylor has the modest advantage over Milton of not making his God a "school-divine." Satan argues; Christ replies with the simple affection of a father. Satan tries all the ambiguities: sin is too slight to bother about, too gross for God to forgive; Grace is "but an airy notion or a name"; doubtful phantasms are the existence of God, of Heaven, and of Hell.

But Taylor reserves his subtler analysis for the dialogues between the soul of the convert and the 'saint,' the more experienced Christian, who knows the sophistries of Satan and the growing-pains of the regenerate. The Soul suffers from scrupulosities: it fears that only fear of Hell, not love of God, motivates it; it fears "under each Duty done, Hypocrisy"; it is troubled by the philosophical objection that the Christian God is but "a Heape of Contradictions high"; it is disturbed by the misconduct of professed Christians. Finally the saint succeeds in reassuring the novice that the devout life is struggle and gradual progress, and the piece ends with seven lyrics expressive of spiritual triumph and rapture. It is characteristic of Taylor's nature (as everywhere discovered in his poetry) that the drama concerns itself with the souls of the elect: this Puritan poet nowhere contemplates the situation of the damned or touches his lips to the minatory trumpet.

The problem of the 'long poem' presents itself all simply to Taylor. He probably never saw *Paradise Lost,* published the year before he left England; his instances would be *The Divine Weeks, Christ's Victory,* and *The Purple Island,* Anne

Bradstreet's *Four Elements*. Within his scope were the sustained allegory of Phineas Fletcher or the graceful Spenserian texture of Giles or the simple, unfigured, unpretentious Tudor verse of the Tenth Muse; but he elected none of them. The piece suggests drama, though it attempts no adjustment of speech to speaker. Of course, Spenser and Milton make none either; but then there is an epic style to be established, a style consistent in its elegance or opulence. The conceitist method, admirably suited either to the lyric, which it provides with initial structure, or to the short piece, satiric or elegiac, in which constant metaphoric explosion can operate brilliantly, is ill suited to the continuum of the epic or the dramatic. Taylor did not attempt it as seriously as did Du Bartas. Only the lyrics within *Determinations* have tolerable poetic success: the dialogue and narrative oscillate between unreconciled manners in a fashion not to have been tolerated by Giles Fletcher. Without adjustment, the style is now rhetorical or juristic, now colloquial; the diction now theologic, now provincial. Unaware of the stratifications in his vocabulary, Taylor does not know how to expose them with intent and for an effect. And his handling of the trope has equal uncertainty. The "Effects of Mans Apostacy," the first section, opens with an extended if not very original conceit of sin storming the fortress of the heart, which is pursued, with tolerable application, for something like thirty lines, then dropped for straight narrative. There follows a Dantean simile, quite alien in tone and technique:

> Then like a Child that fears the Poker Clapp
> Him on his face doth on his Mothers lap
> Doth hold his breath, lies still for fear least hee
> Should by his breathing lowd discover'd bee.....

Taylor is seen to better advantage in his lyrics, within and without the *Determinations*. Between 1682 and 1715 he composed over two hundred "Sacramental Meditations" (of which Johnson's selection prints thirty-one). It was the poet's custom to celebrate the Lord's Supper about five times a year and to write for each observance a poem based upon some passage of Scripture. Though the majority of the texts are taken from the Gospels, more than seven come from the Song of Songs, which Taylor, following the traditional practice of Christendom and the immediate precedent of Quarles in Book IV of his *Emblems,* interprets allegorically.

A better than average example of his lyrics is "Meditation Eight," from the Johannine hint, "I am the living bread."

> I kenning through Astronomy Divine
>> The Worlds bright Battlement, wherein I spy
> A Golden Path my Pensill cannot line
>> From that bright Throne unto my Threshold ly.
>> And while my puzzled thoughts about it pore,
>> I find the Bread of Life in't at my doore.
>
> When that this Bird of Paradise put in
>> This Wicker Cage (my Corps) to tweedle praise
> Had peckt the Fruite forbid: and so did fling
>> Away its Food, and lost its golden dayes,
>> It fell into Celestiall Famine sore,
>> And never could attain a morsell more.
>
> Alas! Alas! Poore Bird, what wilt thou doe?
>> This Creatures field no food for Souls e're gave:
> And if thou knock at Angells dores, they show
>> An Empty Barrell: they no soul bread have.
>> Alas! Poore Bird, the Worlds White Loafe is done,
>> And cannot yield thee here the smallest Crumb.

In this sad state, Gods Tender Bowells run
  Out streams of Grace: And he to end all strife,
The Purest Wheate in Heaven, his deare-dear Son
  Grinds, and kneads up into this Bread of Life.
  Which Bread of Life from Heaven down came and stands
  Disht in thy Table up by Angells Hands.

Did God mould up this Bread in Heaven, and bake,
  Which from his Table came, and to thine goeth?
Doth he bespeake thee thus: This Soule Bread take;
  Come, Eate thy fill of this, thy Gods White Loafe?
  Its Food too fine for Angells; yet come, take
  And Eate thy fill! Its Heavens Sugar Cake.

What Grace is this knead in this Loafe? This thing
  Souls are but petty things it to admire.
Yee Angells, help: This fill would to the brim
  Heav'ns whelm'd-down Chrystall meele Bowle, yea and higher,
  This Bread of Life dropt in thy mouth doth Cry:
  Eate, Eate me, Soul, and thou shalt never dy.

Taylor's curious coupling of "thing" and "brim," matched in other poems, shows not only that he did not sound terminal *g* but that he accounted nasals a satisfactory rhyme; and elsewhere he allows loose consonances and assonances to count as rhyme. These latitudes share with his Warwickshire provincialisms, his downright coinages, his inversions and other awkward, sometimes unconstruable constructions (like that in the opening stanza) in giving to this poem and his others a primitive vigor and naïveté irrelevant to the baroque aesthetic and unparalleled in other 'metaphysical' verse of the period.

Donne's celebrated prosody in the Satires, like that of other free writers of pentameter iambic, provides its approximate pattern by offering, in a line, either five strong stresses, without calculation of weak syllables, or ten syllables, without calculation of stresses, trusting that the two latitudes will balance to a conversational verse. But Taylor, though he had an iambic rhythm in his memory, seems chiefly to have counted the syllables; and his characteristic practice is to write a line slowed up by its extra stresses. "They no soul bread have" requires an equal weight to each syllable. The line of monosyllables, "What Grace is this knead in this Loafe? This thing," is best read as spondaic. Like other poets, ancient and contemporary, who reduce the flexible music of their rhythms, Taylor compensates by supplying rather copious alliteration—not as structure but as pure and simple phonetic pleasure.

The stiffness of Taylor's lines must not be attributed merely to prosodic awkwardness. Unquestionably he preferred a packed line; like greater poets—Donne, Hopkins, and Crane he was impatient of space given to prepositions and articles and other poetic neutralities. Taylor's "Heav'ns whelm'd-down Chrystall meele Bowle" is less rare in kind for him than, for George Herbert, is the "Christ-side-piercing Spear" of "Prayer."

The poem, which in spite of its inversions seems modern, has the force of its compression, its density. But its chief character is its metaphorism. Taylor is capable—one sees from "The Ebb and Flow" and "Huswifery"—of working out, neatly and precisely, a conceit: the latter poem tidily analogizes the Christian life to all the instruments and processes of cloth-making—the spinning wheel, the distaff, the reel, the loom, the web, the fulling mills, until the robes of salvation are ready for the pious wearing. Such poems, better called short allegories than extended conceits, are, however, less typical of Taylor and poetically less impressive than the poem before us, of which the method, more bold, is less surely prosecuted.

"Meditation Eight" has the advantage of ending with its two best stanzas. Taylor begins uncertain of direction and with trite locutions (like "golden path" and "bright throne"), locutions bad exactly in the wrong way for baroque poetry. Then the bird figure occurs to him: the soul is bird of Paradise in a double sense—child of heaven and heir of Eden's Adam, who was put in the 'cage' of the Garden as the Soul has been put into that of the Body, to sing God's praises, but who (like his descendant soul) has instead eaten of the forbidden fruit. Taylor manages this equivalence neatly for three lines: the "wicker" cage can well stand for the tree-shaded garden; "peckt" properly modifies bird as well as man. But after that he has his difficulties: while, for a stanza more, evoking the soul as bird, he has really ceased thinking in terms of the figure, without knowing how to return to the narrative "I" of the first stanza; and, before he shapes the "I" into a "thou," he takes in transit a scriptural enough figure of God's running bowels which, however scriptural, is too strong a trope to be thrust, briefly and unsignificantly, into a poem with its own central boldness. "To end all Strife" seems pure aid to the rhyme, since (though there is famine) no conflict has been mentioned.

Then, happily, Taylor finds his tone and theme, already sounded (under the accidental protection of the 'bird') in the third stanza: the translation of Supersubstantial Bread, the *panis angelicus,* into domestic and animistic terms. Even in the last stanzas, the method is too libertine for Donne or Herbert; but the devices associate themselves, in baroque fashion, about surprises—surprises of bearing down with a poet's literalness upon the propositions that Christ is the Bread (therefore subject to all the accidents and comparisons to which bread is subject). The total effect of the poem is amateurish but—by virtue of persistent episodic interest and a theme most efficiently defined as the poem nears its end—powerful.

"The Reflexion," upon the text, "I am the rose of Sharon," is a brilliant piece. In accordance with Taylor's frequent fashion, each stanza is allotted its own conceit, while the textual image, the rose, appears and reappears.

> Once at thy Feast, I saw thee Pearle-like stand
>   'Tween Heaven and Earth, where Heavens Bright glory all
> In streams fell on thee, as a floodgate and,
>   Like Sun Beams through thee on the World to Fall.
>   Oh! Sugar sweet then! My Deare sweet Lord, I see
>   Saints Heaven-lost Happiness restor'd by thee.
>
> Shall Heaven and Earth's bright Glory all up lie,
>   Like Sun Beams bundled in the sun in thee?
> Dost thou sit Rose at Table Head, where I
>   Do sit, and Carv'st no morsell sweet for mee?
>   So much before, so little now! Sprindge, Lord,
>   Thy Rosie Leaves, and me their Glee afford.

Christ, as the Rose, offers his sacramental presence; he "sits Rose at Table Head" and carves a morsel of what is at once meat, bread, flower, and supreme value. Sometimes we can visualize Taylor's conceit, after the fashion of an Italian or Flemish primitive, in two or three strong colors against a flat gold background, or of a seventeenth-century 'emblem,' an engraving which literally translates into graphic terms a literary figure: so one can read the Pearl, through which sun-

beams stream down upon a terrestrial globe; so one can read
the opening of another poem of Taylor's, a 'song of innocence':

> My shattered Phancy stole away from mee
> (Wits run a Wooling over Edens Parke)
> And in Gods Garden saw a golden Tree,
>> Whose Heart was All Divine, and gold its barke:
>> Whose glorious limbs and fruitfull branches strong
>> With Saints and Angells bright are richly hung.

But "Dost thou sit Rose" is more complex: it at once invites
and repels visualization. Exciting by its compression, it is,
and is not, connected with the figures which precede and
follow it. Is the preceding "thee," compact with bright
glories, the anthropomorphic figure of Christ as the Rose?
Whichever, it is difficult not to avoid a connotative over-
lapping of Christ, the Rose, and the Sun of Righteousness:
"in the sun in thee" consists of two disjunct phrases, one of
which goes with "bundled," the other with "lie," but juxtaposed as they are, one takes "thee" also as appositive of "sun."
And then in the last couplet, have we left the Table for the
Garden? The answer has to be indecisive, for the "rosie
leaves" equate the "sweet morsels" of the sacred feast,
yet the figure of distribution takes a new and garden turn:
"sprindge" (spread) your leaves, and spreading them share
with me their "Glee"—their joy, mirth, music. The "rosie
leaves" must be the petals: the rose is to open, tendering its
petals and their glee, which is perhaps first their equivalence
of music, their "sugar sweet" fragrance, then their spiritual
delight, their mystical joy. Thus to explicate the stanza is to
show Taylor's fancy moving playfully in a mode nearer to
symbolisme than to the logical prosecution of a conceit.

Something like seven of Taylor's poems have whole virtue; of the others, there are few without a signal stanza or a brilliant line. The work is very uneven; exciting to look into, disappointing to read with consecutive patience. The equivalent can be said of *Theophila*'s Edward Benlowes; of Du Bartas and his translator, Sylvester. Conceitist poetry is never simply commonplace. Bad classical poetry is worn, threadbare, insipid; bad baroque poetry is either a succession of labored ingenuities or a series of uncontrolled conflagrations, spasmodic eruptions, meaningless violences: its worst is a kind of coldly calculated fury. Taylor is sometimes a neat little artisan but more often an unsteady enthusiast, a naïve original, an intermittently inspired Primitive. He is rarely uninteresting, on some level; but his taste—and there is a baroque taste as well as a classical—is unschooled, unsteady. Even Cleveland has taste—of an equilibristic sort: he moves at the pitch of keen intellectual vaudeville; he is a kind of erudite version of the *New Yorker*'s poets. But Taylor is nearer to being an ancestor of another uneven village poet, Emily Dickinson.

Of the poets with whom Taylor invokes comparison— Crashaw, Blake, Dickinson, Hopkins, Crane—all are greater and all are frequent and more sure in their successes. But it is enough to say of Taylor that, like the others, he is at worst still a poet.

1941

II

GEORGE HERBERT

EVEN without benefit of Ruskin's antithetic descriptions
—his St. Mark's at Venice, magnificent in its marble
and gold, yet fronted by a *piazza* swarming with children
and beggars; his English cathedral, neat, trim, surrounded
by closely clipped lawns perambulated by starched nurse-
maids—one could trust himself to feel the difference between the two worlds. Chartres, Notre Dame at Paris, St.
Peter's at Rome—all are show places freely open to tourists,
who wander about in aimless amazement or pedantic bore-
dom or dissenting incomprehension or aesthetic reverie; but,
at altars high and low, masses go on all morning; before
shrines and votive candles the pious pray, undisturbed by
Anglo-Saxon curiosity. Still the houses of God, not relics of
some former and alien age, Continental churches rarely re-
nounce the pious offerings aesthetically so distasteful—the
wax or paper flowers, or cheap lace frontals; crutches, or
limbs in wax effigy, deposited by men grateful to therapeutic saints.

In contrast, the English cathedral almost universally seems
a museum piece, cherished and kept in faithful repair by impulses respectful, filial, antiquarian, British—but not specifically religious. Where, before the Reformation, altars once
stood, the wall boasts, as everywhere, its spotless whitewash;

but, neatly attached to the wall, a decanal placard supplies accurate historical information. From the incursions of schoolboys and tourists there is decently withdrawn, for "prayer and meditation," one chapel—where a pious lady or two may, without embarrassment, say her collects. All is neat and orderly; the restorations have been executed, under the supervision of that learned historian, the Dean, by the best modern experts. All bespeaks the church as by law established; can these legal, dry bones live?

From the cathedrals and the city temples of Wren one must turn to village churches, more appropriately reached by cycle than by motor. Two of England's holiest places are so small as to hold scarcely fifty worshipers; both owe their modest repute and their sanctity to saints of the Anglican golden age—the seventeenth century. At Little Gidding, in Huntingtonshire, Nicholas Ferrar established, with a membership recruited solely from his own kinsfolk, his "Protestant Nunnery," a retreat visited by the Cambridge poet, Crashaw, and by his sacred majesty, Charles the Martyr. At Bemerton, a mile from Salisbury, Ferrar's friend, George Herbert, passed his final three years.

The "almost incredible story" of his rectorate has been told by Izaak Walton. In an age of clerical laxity, Herbert, accompanied by his household, read matins and evensong daily at the "canonical hours" of ten and four. Many gentlemen of the neighborhood attended these offices; and "some of the meaner sort of his parish did so love and reverence Mr. Herbert that they would let their plough rest when Mr. Herbert's saint's bell rung to prayers, that they might also offer their devotions to God with him, and would then return back to their plough." Skilled at music and accustomed to set his simpler poems to music, singing them to his lute, Herbert twice weekly walked into Salisbury to attend choral service at the cathedral and, thereafter, to play and sing his part at a gathering of amateur music-makers. Upon one of these walks, Herbert encountered a poor man whose battered horse had fallen under its load; and, putting off his canonical coat, he relieved the distress of man and beast. His musical friends expressed surprise at the soiled clothing of one customarily so trim and spotless; and one rebuked him for forgetting his dignity of birth and office. Herbert answered that "the thought of what he had done would prove music to him at midnight, and that the omission of it would have upbraided and made discord in his conscience. . . . . And now let us tune our instruments."

Not always had Herbert been so subdued to Christian humility. His ancestry was distinguished: on his father's side he descended from a line of valorous soldiers—suppressors, as royal stewards in the Welsh marches, of rebels, thieves, and outlaws; on his mother's side, from the Talbots, Devereux, and Greys, and many other noble families. His mother, Lady Magdalen, had Donne for devoted friend and, ultimately, for funeral eulogist. George was her fifth son; of the others, the eldest, Lord Edward Herbert of Cherbury, was soldier, diplomat, biographer of his own adventurous career, author of the deistic *De veritate,* a subtle and rare poet; after a learned education, Richard betook himself to Flanders, where he won much reputation both in battle and at dueling, carrying to his Flemish grave the scars of four and twenty wounds; William took his part in the Danish and Flemish wars; Thomas fought in Germany, sailed to the East Indies, served in the King's navy, was valiant in single combat and skilful at dueling, French, and the ways of court; Henry became Master of the Revels, Gentleman of the King's Privy Chamber, and possessor of a luxurious fortune.

Passion and choler were the infirmities of all the Herberts— a strong, ambitious family. George was a proper Herbert. Designs of a military career never possessed him, perhaps because his frail constitution forbade; but by other secular ambitions he was stirred. At sixteen, he entered Trinity College, Cambridge, there to spend the next eighteen years. Though his pious mother had ever intended him for the Anglican priesthood and though at seventeen he wrote her a pair of sonnets renouncing profane love and verse, he shifted ambition to secular preferment. Soon fellow of his college, he was elected in 1620 to the public oratorship of the university; and, encouraged by the course of his predecessors in the office, he hoped one day to become Secretary of State. His learning, wit, and elegance, both of tongue and person, won him the acclaim and the distinguished connections for which, at best, the Orator might hope. When King James bestowed upon the University Library his own volume, *Basilicon Doron,* Herbert made the official reply in a florid and extravagantly flattering letter, the tone of which may be judged from his conclusion: "Peregrinis Academicis nostram invisentibus. Quid Vaticanam Bodleiumque objicis, Hospes? Unicus est nobis Bibliotheca Liber." Properly praised, the learned King judged Herbert "the jewel of that university." Another extant example of Herbert's skill at panegyric—in Latin and Greek—hailed the return of Prince Charles from his unsuccessful Spanish journey; and still another welcomed to Cambridge the ambassadors of his Catholic Majesty, the King of Spain.

During his undergraduate years, it was observed, Herbert dressed with elegance, kept at a distance from his social inferiors, and took pride in his blood and parts. His success as Orator won for him the admiration of Francis Bacon and Lancelot Andrewes and John Donne as well as of powerful nobles. Often leaving the university, he attended the King, following him in his progresses. Says Walton, simply, "With .... his annuity, and the advantage of his college, and of his oratorship, he enjoyed his genteel humor for clothes, and courtlike company, and seldom looked toward Cambridge unless the King was there, but then he never failed."

Anticipating a permanent removal from Cambridge to London, Herbert suffered a check in his secular progress. His most powerful friends, the Duke of Richmond and the Marquis of Hamilton, died; and, shortly after them, the King. In retirement, Herbert weighed his diminished prospects at court, considered again his mother's and his own original intention. The balancing turned into a spiritual conflict, not of flesh against spirit, but of the spirit against pride.

Much to his credit, Herbert did not consider the mere transfer of his ambitions from one profession to another. Most clergymen have been not unfairly delineated in the novels of Austen and Trollope: not worse than other men, not hypocrites or sensualists, they are still not conspicuously better or different in their motivations; they aim to advance their estates, win preferment, to be as palpably successful as their schoolmates who have pursued law or business. Probably only a saint can be expected to say *nolo episcopari;* most clergymen boast no such high vocation.

For Herbert, as for William Law, Anglican saint of the next century, there were two ways of life, discrete, not reconciled. The world esteems energy, valor, breeding, wit, self-respect; but, says *The Country Parson,* "the two highest points of life, wherein a Christian is most seen, are Patience and Mortification." "The Pearl" recalls by its title St. Matthew's merchant who, finding a jewel of great price, sold all that he had in order to buy. In his poem, Herbert described what he surrendered—and for what. The ways of learning, of honor, of pleasure:

> I know all these, and have them in my hand;
> Therefore not sealed, but with open eyes
> I fly to Thee, and fully understand
> Both the main sale, and the commodities;
> And at what rate and price I have thy love.

In the pattern of their lives Herbert and Donne offer a partial parallel. Both had an early devotion to theology; in both it was stifled by secular ambition; both took Orders only when their secular ambition proved frustrate. Yet, like à Becket, who, from being King Henry's merry companion, turned his ecclesiastical judge and foe, both these courtier poets proved capable of decision; and, having decided, they did not look back. Their subsequent years of discipline and devotion demonstrated the sincerity of their resolves.

Upon informing a court friend of his intention, Herbert was urged to alter it, as degrading to his birth and ability. He replied: "Though the iniquity of the late times have made clergymen meanly valued, and the sacred name of priest contemptible, yet I will labor to make it honorable, by consecrating all my learning and all my poor abilities to advance the glory of that God that gave them. . . . . And I will labor to be like my Savior, by making humility lovely in the eyes of all men."

For prudential reasons, Herbert married. He accepted the living of Foulston-cum-Bemerton-Capella, "changed his sword and silk clothes into a canonical coat," and began his cure of souls. Fastidious, he must have found his congregation of rustics a constant irritant and hence a constant spur to self-discipline. He was determined to exact from his countryfolk that decorum in church which reverence demanded: they were not to talk during service, or to sleep or gaze about at their neighbors, or to lean forward or half-kneel at prayers, or to make their responses "in a huddling or slubbering fashion—gaping or scratching the head, or spitting even in the midst of their answer." Nor could he tolerate untidiness in the church; it must be "kept clean, without dust or cobwebs; and, at great festivals, strewed and stuck with boughs, and perfumed with incense."

Except within the church, however, he could allow himself no refinements. He must visit his parishioners as Christian souls, without respect to persons. In his instructions to the country parson, homilies preached first of all to himself, Herbert, recognizing that most men wear their best clothes and their best behavior to church, bids the priest call upon his parishioners when they are "wallowing in the midst of their affairs." In the pursuit of his pastoral office, the priest may not disdain to "enter into the poorest cottage, though he even creep into it, and though it smell never so loathesomely. For both God is there also, and those for whom God died."

From childhood a dweller in London or Cambridge, Herbert sought to adapt himself and his use to his rural parish. At the end of his first sermon—learned and elaborate as if to show his brilliance—he announced his intention thereafter to preach plainly and practically. An admiring friend of Bishop Andrewes, he renounced the ingenious exegetical methods of that great preacher together with his wit, learning, and eloquence; and, finding that simple people, little heedful of exortations, relish and remember stories and sayings, he made use of such bait.

Adages had formed a favorite study with men like Andrewes and John Selden. *Jacula Prudentium, or Outlandish Proverbs,* first published eight years after Herbert's death, was undoubtedly used by its compiler in his parish sermons; and some of these homely maxims may be found in the poems, especially in "The Church Porch." Indeed, this prelude to *The Temple* is a cento of aphorisms which, though assembled into six-line stanzas, might fittingly have been versified in neoclassical couplets; in a couplet, indeed, each stanza ends. "The Church Porch" compends a moral philosophy, classical and popular—such Aristotelian and Stoic thoughts as have passed into the treasury of common sense. By way of humanistic preparation for Christian devotion, Herbert reviews the standards of decency; like Newman in his portrait of a gentleman, he delineates the character generally accepted as the highest—at the level of what the eighteenth century would have called 'natural religion.' Only, Christian humanist that he was, Herbert does not antithesize 'natural' and supernatural virtues. There is, of course, a false wisdom of this world which is, indeed, foolishness with God; but there is also a wisdom which is sound so far as it goes—a classical wisdom which revelation does not abolish but completes. This is the wisdom represented, for the people, in the proverbs of all nations and, for the educated, in the *Analects,* the *Nicomachean Ethics,* and the *De officiis.* In the spirit of this wisdom Herbert commends temperance ("drink not

[26]

the third glass"); the avoidance of smut and profanity; in the management of money, the mean between parsimony and prodigality; the proper use of conversation; and, most centrally and ardently, the virtues of self-examination, self-control, constancy, integration.

> When thou dost purpose aught within thy power
> Be sure to do it, though it be but small:
> Constancy knits the bones and makes us tower
> When wanton pleasures beckon us to thrall.
>> Who breaks his own bond, forfeiteth himself;
>> What nature made a ship, he makes a shelf.
>
> .   .   .   .
>
> Who keeps no guard upon himself is slack
> And rots to nothing at the next great thaw.
> Man is a shop of rules, a well-truss'd pack,
> Whose every parcel underwrites a law.
>> Lose not thyself, nor give thy humors way:
>> God gave them to thee under lock and key.

In *The Country Parson,* Herbert urges the preacher to use examples, especially those drawn from daily life and the experiences habitual with his parishioners; and he remarks that such illustration is in accord with Holy Scripture, which "condescends to the naming of a plough, a hatchet, a bushel, leaven, boys piping and dancing,—showing that things of ordinary use are not only to serve in the way of drudgery, but to be washed and cleansed, and serve for lights even of heavenly truths." Again, discoursing on the Parson's "completeness" as a parish *person,* able to cure the simple legal and medical maladies of his neighbors, Herbert recommends the cultivation of herbs, since these plants will not only prove substitutes for exotic drugs but will supply the parson himself with metaphors. This Christ did in order that "by familiar things he might make his doctrine slip the more easily into the hearts even of the meanest" and especially that "laboring people, whom he chiefly considered, might have everywhere monuments of his doctrine; remembering in gardens his mustard-seed and lilies, in the fields his seed corn and tares." The servant is not above his master.

None of Herbert's parish homilies survives. But even when writing for himself, not for "laboring people," he uses such analogies as they would apprehend. "The Country Parson, as soon as he awakes on Sunday, presently falls to work, and seems to himself so as a marketman is when the market day comes, or a shopkeeper when customers use to come in. His thoughts are full of making the best of the day, and contriving it to his best gains." In *The Temple,* too, homely analogies and illustrations prevail.

> Who sweeps a room, as for Thy laws,
> Makes that and th' action fine.

The constant man is he

> Who rides his sure and even trot
> While the world now rides by, now lags behind.

Sunday, Christ set aside for men's spiritual life

> That as each beast his manger knows
> Man might not of his fodder miss.

In God's love, "more than in bed, I rest."

Were Herbert's poems, then, deliberately written for the unlearned, the 'workers'? Presumably not. *The Temple* is Herbert's spiritual autobiography; dying, he left it to his friend, Nicholas Ferrar, to determine whether it should appear: "if he think it may turn to the advantage of any dejected poor soul, let it be made public; if not, let him burn it." But surely *The Country Parson* provides the best commentary on *The Temple*. And, surely, the Christian discipline of his pride may well have led Herbert to write such poems as might speak to all. What is the meaning of his two poems with the common title, "Jordan"? Perhaps he recalled the Syrian Naaman who, bidden by Elisha to wash in the Jordan and be cleansed of his leprosy, cried out, affronted, "Are not Abana and Pharpar, rivers of Damascus, better than all the waters of Israel?" Fuller says of Quarles that he "drank of Jordan instead of Helicon, and slept on Mount Olivet for his Parnassus"; and the antithesis of rival founts and mounts recurs elsewhere. The theme of both poems is evident. Though secular verse may need adornment—nightingales and purling streams, metaphors and invention—not so with sacred poetry: "Shepherds are honest people; let them sing." That drinking of the Jordan was an ascetic practice seems the judgment of Lord Herbert of Cherbury, who, acknowledging the sanctity of his brother's last years, thinks his English poems "far short of expressing those perfections he had in the Greek and Latin tongues."

Herbert does not eschew the 'literary' merely in his metaphors. His diction is that of the English Bible: habitually, as Coleridge has called it, "pure, manly, and unaffected." His syntax rarely admits inversion or any other mode of poetic dislocation; his sentence structure is that of good conversation—though firm, yet supple and easy.

From his secular youth Herbert allowed two aesthetic devotions to survive: his love of music and his love of order. Music is an audible rehearsal of order. What is a dissonance but a tone alien to the chordal triad? Harmony weaves individual voices into the pattern of a society. Herbert's favorite metaphor, that of tuning the lute, symbolizes the adjustment of strayed strings to the pitch of the constant, or of all the strings to some objective standard. Since the lute stood in constant need of such attention, it aptly paralleled the unstable nature of man. Herbert's poems portray, as he said, "the many spiritual conflicts that have passed betwixt God and my soul"; but he identifies the end of religion as the submission of man's will to God's.

Certain kinds of external order attracted Herbert's temperament: he liked hierarchy in church and state, the prescription of a common liturgy. For his poetry, he devised intricate stanza patterns; and, having initiated a pattern, he maintained it throughout the poem. It is Order which gives

> All things their set forms and hours,
> Makes of wild woods sweet walks and bowers.

Art is the ordering of landscapes and loves. By the obvious kinds of spontaneity Herbert was not tempted.

His conflicts lay deeper. Religion is, in essence, the reduction to order of the human will. The mark of that effected order is peace. Wondering how those lowest in Paradise can lack restless desire, Dante is assured by one of these spirits that if they desired a higher place, their wills would be discordant from that of God: *la sua volontate è nostra pace.* Yet more than of poetry, the line is a touchstone of spiritual direction. False prophets, of religion as well as of culture, are ever promising some labor-saving device, some formula for getting rich or learned without toil, wise or holy without discipline. Like Fénélon, Herbert never betrays us to such delusion. He sees human life—its inconstancy (our "twenty several selves"), the insatiability of its desires; and, in "The Pulley," he represents God as having endowed man with beauty, wisdom, honor, pleasure, reserving, as the divine gift, only peace. To effect this inner order, this submission of his will to God's, Herbert endured those conflicts which the poems re-enact.

Occasionally Herbert seeks to incarnate the theme of a poem in its very form. "Denial," with its five-line pattern, leaves the last line unrhymed until the final stanza, when the soul, before "untuned, unstrung," attains to unison with God's harmony. In "Grief," verses are bidden to keep their measures for some lover

> Whose grief allows him music and a rhyme;
> For mine excludes both measure, tune, and time.
> —Alas, my God.

The rhymeless, truncated last line exemplifies the breakdown. In "Home," written on the Advent, the last stanza practices a similar adaptation. The poem on Trinity Sunday uses three-line stanzas; "The Altar" and "Easter Wings" visualize the objects they signify.

These innocent ingenuities have been duly chastised in Addison's essay on "False Wit" and elsewhere in neoclassical criticism. Relatively few in number, they proceed from a principle analogous to onomatopoeia and equally harmless in moderation: the expressive adjustment of structure, phonetic or typographical, to theme.

Most of Herbert's poetry is conventionally, though variously, patterned: of his one hundred and sixty-nine poems, one hundred and sixteen are composed in stanza forms which are not repeated. Having sacrificed learned allusion and poetic diction, having adopted a conversational syntax, Herbert could still, with pure conscience, retain the art of metrical invention. In Herbert's stanzaic invention, as in the constant precision of his craftsmanship, there survives his temperamental fastidiousness. The tension between inner struggle and outer neatness gives its central character to his poetry.

Herbert's instrument is delicate of timbre and limited of gamut; not the sustainedly sonorous organ nor the imperious

> tuba, mirum spargens sonum
> per sepulcra regionum

but viol or lute, apt for accompaniment, adjusted to the chamber and the closet. Moderate in pitch, its tone can, without hysterical tightening, rise to joy and, avoiding the whine and the sob, sink to pathos. This control of scale, this restrained modulation, are the natural concomitants of a remarkable poetic integrity. Whether or not he learned his architecture from Donne, Herbert composes a lyric as a whole; and he should be quoted not by lines or by stanzas but by poems. Brilliant phrases there are, of course, like "church bells beyond the stars heard," in that brilliant and tender poem, "Prayer."

> Prayer—the church's banquet; angels' age;
>   God's breath in man returning to his birth;
> The soul in paraphrase; heart in pilgrimage;
>   The Christian plummet, sounding heav'n and earth;
>
> Engine against th' Almighty; sinner's tower;
>   Reversed thunder; Christ-side-piercing spear;
> The six-day-world transposing in an hour;
>   A kind of tune, which all things hear and fear;
>
> Softness, and peace, and joy, and love, and bliss;
>   Exalted manna; gladness of the best;
>   Heaven in ordinary; man well drest;

The milky way; the bird of paradise;
  Church bells beyond the stars heard; the soul's blood;
  The land of spices; something understood.

It remains true, however, that the verse which, in its context and as climax, moves the reader cannot be detached; for it is by virtue of its position in the whole poem and as pervaded by what has gone before that it acquires this light and warmth. In some of Herbert's miniatures, the finale—like Milton's in "Lycidas" and *Paradise Lost*—is a diminuendo. The vigor of "The Collar" expounds dramatically the motives to rebellion; the motive to submission finds utterance in but one tender word, the acknowledgment of submission in two more.

Through the influence of Coleridge in England and Emerson in America, Herbert did not want, in the nineteenth century, for readers capable of some justice to his spirit and to his art; in addition to this audience of the 'literary,' he continued to reach the devout, for whom *The Temple* took its place with the Bible, the Book of Common Prayer, Law's *Serious Call,* and Keble's *The Christian Year*. These nineteenth-century audiences have dispersed; but Herbert has survived many changes in doctrine and poetic mode. With our own time, the reaction against romantic and Victorian poetry has led to a revaluation of the seventeenth-century lyric. Donne, restored to something like the position he held for his own generation, has drawn attention and study to those other introspective poets, commonly called 'metaphysical,' who followed him.

Donne's program excluded mythological and other 'literary' decoration. For conventional, hyperbolic laud of love and mistress, he substituted realistic but subtle analysis of the experienced. Resolved to transfer the whole of himself to his verses, he saw no reason to deny or conceal his erudition in geography, astronomy, physiology, the dialectic of the Schools. He drew his analogies from his own universe of discourse and illustrated love from science. Chiefly Donne sought to make poetry out of reasoning—not *de rerum natura* but about his own problems. Yet versified analysis is not poetry; to escape being metered prose, poetry must either relieve its statements by images or think in images. A poet's simile may not advance his thought but merely illustrate it. But Donne made an endeavor, at which he was frequently successful, to have analysis move *pari passu* with metaphor. His characteristic device was a protracted 'conceit,' disclosing successive but interpenetrating points of likeness between the objects relationally identified. Thus Christ, between Good Friday and Easter,

> For these three days became a mineral.
> He was all gold when He lay down, but rose
> All tincture, and doth not alone dispose
> Leaden and iron wills to good, but is
> Of power to make e'en sinful flesh like his.

In such a passage the prose meaning and the metaphor are not disjunct, as text and application, but coalesce.

Donne's poetic achievement was not only uneven but in large measure based upon a personality and incapable of full transference, as method, to other and alien temperaments. He united erudition, an introspective and casuistical intelligence, and range of experience with an imaginative intensity often sufficient to fuse these ingredients. To trace the influence of that complex person and poet upon his juniors is to trace an influence which, like a comprehensive will, breaks up the estate into many and various legacies.

His close reasoning, amorous casuistry, and syntax—those long sentences parenthetically interrupted—reappear only in Lord Herbert of Cherbury. Carew, a poet still underestimated, not only wrote the best contemporary analysis of Donne's style but achieved, with a less complex nature and a less dissonant music, some distinguished love poetry of a sort impossible without Donne's predecession. In no really significant sense is Crashaw a 'metaphysical': Giles Fletcher and Marino supply the plausible paternity; his mind, though perverse, is simple; his syntax lacks involution; characteristic images are sensual not scientific. Traherne, an overrated discovery, completely wants Donne's grasp of the poem as a tightly woven pattern; he sprawls. Save for "The Night," Vaughan composed few poems; capable of extraordinary lines and arresting inaugurations, he ordinarily cannot organize or sustain. What chiefly gives these poets their legitimate connection with the name of Donne is their production not of hymns, justifications of Deity, metrical paraphrases of Scripture and Creed, but of autobiographical lyrics in analysis of religious experience.

George Herbert's relation to Donne seems to have been personal rather than literary. Sometimes attributed to Donne are his surrender of the mythological allusions frequent in his Latin poems, his structural neatness, his 'conceits.'

> Only a sweet and virtuous soul,
>   Like seasoned timber, never gives,
> But, though the whole world turn to coal,
>   Then chiefly lives.

Yet the student of *The Country Parson* will be aware of alternative explanations for these traits. *The Temple,* written chiefly during the years at Bemerton, rarely draws its meta-

[35]

phors from travel, science, or philosophy. Herbert's "seasoned timber" offers a shock not because the simile is researched but because, unexpectedly, it juxtaposes the world of ethics and the world of the carpenter.

That he should approach Herbert through Donne is a proper procedure for the literary historian but not necessary for the reader of poetry. There are eighteenth-century essays in blank verse—like Dyer's *Fleece* and Akenside's *Pleasures of the Imagination*—which become intelligible only when we know their Miltonic lineage; when we are possessed of that knowledge, *Paradise Lost* shames them into the status of period pieces. But Herbert's poetry evokes no comparison with epic or dramatic grandeur and, put beside Donne's, is seen to have its own 'end'—as coherent and 'pure' as Donne's, but other.

1936

III

ALEXANDER POPE

NEOCLASSICAL theory of poetry and neoclassical poetry imperfectly agree. This discrepancy is most simply accounted for by remembering that the period called, in literary and aesthetic history, 'neoclassical' is, in philosophical and cultural history, the age of the Enlightenment—the age, that is, of rationalism.

Some bold spirits, impatient of adjustment, were willing to enter heaven at the loss of an eye: in the celebrated quarrel over the relative merits of the Ancients and the Moderns, the modernists firmly took their stand on the achievements of the natural sciences and on social progress, rejecting much ancient literature, notably Homer, as obsolete, childish stuff, compounded of immoral gods, absurd miracles, and primitive manners. The classicists—likely to be either men of letters or churchmen—were necessarily less neat in their position; for, though sharing with their contemporaries the desire to be sensible, enlightened, and modern, they also genuinely admired the achievements of ages unlike their own. Hence their creed often formalizes past moments in literary history, while their practice is very much of their own time.

Thus, while the Enlightenment reinforces the impetus of the *Georgics* and the Horatian epistles toward literature as instruction, the orthodox neoclassical creed still runs: the

epic and the tragedy are the highest genres. Dryden praises
the Georgics for showing what virtuosity can do in making
poetry out of the most unpromising stuff (*"opus superbat
materiam"*); but in his own works he distinguishes between
the *sermo pedestris* of such ratiocinative essays as *Religio laici*
and his 'poetry,' a distinction not invalidated by the customary
real superiority of his 'lower' over his 'higher' style. When
Pope says, I "stoop to truth and moralize my song," he is
not wholly ironic.

Neoclassical poems are likely to conform to Cartesian criteria for truth—clarity and distinctness; and the poet is likely
to be a well-educated, methodical, and elegant expositor of
accepted ethical generalizations. But neoclassical criticism
continues to employ a terminology important parts of which
are ultimately referable to Plato: words like 'invention'
(creative imagination), 'inspiration,' 'fire,' and 'poetic fury.'
Like Enlightened Christians who, though retaining the word
'revelation,' are centrally concerned to show that theirs is a
reasonable religion, the poet-critics use language difficult to
reconcile with their performance or thin down and rationalize
the old terms. Thus Johnson dismissed, as mere commonplace, Young's conjectural exhortation to literary originality;
and Pope's preface to Homer exalts 'invention' and 'fire' above
all the strategies of literary intelligence; yet neoclassical poetry
lacks that large boldness it praises. It praises what it cannot
really imitate.

The poets and critics were partially aware of this situation.
Unlike the simpler modernists, they found a characteristic
adjustment in a double standard of loss and gain, progress
and decadence, an advance in refinement, a diminution of
vigor. "Our numbers were in their nonage till Waller and

Denham" has to be reconciled with the humble acknowledgment of "giant wits before the Flood." Walsh's famous advice to Pope must not be taken too simply; it really means: the great things are done; the age of myth-making is over; what remains to be done is to achieve that "correctness," that nicety of detail, which bolder writers and bolder ages perforce neglect.

Attempting to reconcile Homer and Shakespeare with Hobbes and Locke, the poets found themselves handicapped. The dramatists—Wycherly, Congreve, Dryden (in *All for Love,* which, and not *Cato,* gives us a conception of good neoclassical tragedy)—fared best, though English classicism suffers for want of a tragic genius comparable to Racine's. Milton's epic is not easy to locate in literary history; but, written by a poet versed in the Italian and French critics, praised as well as 'tagged' by Dryden, demonstrated by Addison to be a 'regular' epic, admired by Pope as well as by Dennis and Gildon, *Paradise Lost* may be regarded as England's neoclassical epic. After *Paradise Lost,* however, epic poetry loses virtue in both France and England, though it is still to be essayed by the ambitions of Blackmore, Glover, and Voltaire. As Pope's ironic recipe for writing on epic implies, a series of technical devices drawn by generalization from the accredited masterpieces is inadequate unless there is an epic spirit—perhaps he would have added, if properly questioned, "and a heroic age."

The idea of the Great Poem, of the Great Genius, of the (often correlated) Grand Style intimidated many Augustan poets, "froze the genial current" of their souls. Only, it seems, if they could say to themselves, "This is of course not poetry, or not *really great* poetry," could they have a fair chance of writing it. Thus Prior, though himself proud of his epic-didactic *Solomon,* his certification that he is a 'major' poet, is really sure of his tone, really poetic only in his fables and songs and mock-didactic *Alma.* "Rural Elegance: An Ode" and its companion odes and elegies are negligible exercises; but let Shenstone suppose himself to be writing "levities," and he moves toward poetry. Intending a burlesque of Spenser, he is free to write imaginatively of his childhood. More violent ways of emancipating one's self from the censorship of reason were those of Chatterton and Macpherson, both of whom found pseudonymous personalities through which to express their censorable selves. Chatterton, whose public self held the atheist and republican views of a 'man of reason' and wrote able satire ("Kew Gardens"), created, for his more imaginative self, the *persona* of a fifteenth-century Catholic priest. The two kinds of verse written by Christopher Smart, in and out of his mind, instance another split.

The most successful reconciliation of classicism and rationalism, or poetry and philosophy, or the incorrect, great past and the neater, thinner present, took place in terms of burlesque. Burlesque is often mask, often humility. The mock-epic is not mockery of the epic but elegantly affectionate homage, offered by a writer who finds it irrelevant to his age. As its signal advantage, burlesque (with its allied forms, satire and irony) allows a self-conscious writer to attend to objects, causes, and persons in which he is deeply interested yet of which, in part or with some part of him, he disapproves. 'Interest' is a category which subsumes love and hate, approval and disapproval; very often it is an unequal, an unsteady mixture. Burlesque covers a multitude of adjustments;

[40]

and each specimen requires to be separately scrutinized and defined.

Gay's *Shepherd's Week* is one of the clearer cases. Written at Pope's request, it was intended to exhibit the disgustingly crude manners and speech of genuine rustics and so, by reverse, to vindicate Pope's 'Vergilian' pastorals against Phillips' wobblingly 'natural' ones. Actually, however, it exhibits the unsteadiness of Gay's own feelings. We have Johnson's testimony that contemporary readers felt, like us, that most of Gay's shots had hit an unintended target. Without meaning to betray Pope's cause—indeed imagining that he indorsed it—he discovered in the writing the division of his emotional loyalties and discovered, in that division, his attachment to folkways and rural pieties.

In the mock-genres (as well as in the satire and the epistle) it was possible to escape the stylistic restrictions of Great Poetry—its avoidance of "low" terms, its aim at consistent dignity and elegance. It was possible to shift, honorably, from the Beautiful to the Characteristic.

Pope's development followed, in general, this line—from the elegantly decorative to the richly—even the grotesquely—expressive. His poetry is not so homogeneous as its virtual confinement to couplets has often suggested. We should differentiate the *Pastorals,* the Homer, *Eloisa* (which is not only an Ovidian "heroic epistle" but a soliloquy from tragedy, in the manner of Racine), the essays on *Criticism* and on *Man,* the satires and epistles, and the mock-epics. Pope's contemporaries did not confuse them or like them equally. Joseph Warton was not the only reader to think that in *Eloisa* and the *Elegy* Pope showed himself capable of the Pathetic and to regret his turning from this mode to satire. Nor did Coleridge, in the next 'age,' fail to distinguish between the Homer (to which he assigned the chief responsibility for the poetic diction of the eighteenth century) and the satires (composed in such words as a Lake Reformer might have used).

The two pieces, early and late, which give the measure of Pope's development are the *Pastorals,* written before he was eighteen, and the *Dunciad,* which appeared in its enlarged and final form the year before his death.

The *Pastorals* once seemed a monument to poetic 'progress.' In testimony to his admirer, Spence, Pope judged them "the most correct in the versification and musical in the numbers" of all his works; and Warton, in an estimate echoed by Johnson, finds their merit in their "correct and musical versification, musical to a degree of which rhyme could hardly be thought capable, and in [their] giving the first specimen of that harmony in English verse which is now become indispensably necessary." These are technical estimates, specifically of prosody. The *Pastorals* offer evidence of other care and contrivance: they combine as many traditional motifs as possible (e.g., the elegy, the singing match); they profess—in contraction and enrichment of Spenser's precedent—to traverse the four seasons, the four times of day, the four ages of man. Demonstrably superior to Phillips' rival pieces—now turgidly elegant, now rustically English, now plain childish—Pope's stylized pastorals consistently exclude realism.

> See what delight in sylvan scenes appear!
> Descending Gods have found Elysium here.
> In woods bright Venus with Adonis strayed,
> And chaste Diana haunts the forest-shade.

In an early letter Pope explains his prosodic aims in terms suggestive of a 'pure' poetry. The principle of delightful variation is conceived of syllabically and as one might conceive of it if one were writing a string quartet. Indeed Pope's initial aim amounts to a precise working within strict quasi-musical forms. Characteristic canons concern the artful shifting of the caesura, the prohibition of the Alexandrine and the triplet rhyme—indulgences which weaken, by relaxing, the triumph of variation within the confines of twenty syllables. The rules sound mechanical; but the poet who wrote them trusted, confidently, to his ear: "One must," he said to Spence, "tune each line over in one's head to try whether they go right or not."

That the "great rule of verse is to be musical" Pope would never deny—assuming, however, that there are more kinds of music than the sweetness of pastoral verse and the majesty of heroic; he could even distinguish "softness" from "sweetness." Whether in blame or praise, eighteenth-century critics often tagged Pope as "sweet" or "smooth," or "melodious," as though his work were all of a texture. But Pope claimed: "I have followed the significance of the numbers, and the adapting them to the sense, much more even than Dryden; and much oftener than any one minds it"—that is, not only in the set pieces. He liked to recollect a showy couplet from his juvenile and discarded epic:

> Shields, helms, and swords all jangle as they hang
> And sound formidinous with angry clang.

Such an instance, however, makes Pope's notion of "representative harmony" appear limited to the stunt-effects of Poe's "Bells" or Lindsay's "Congo" or his own and Dryden's Cecilian correlations of poetry and music. Nor is Pope helpful to a subtle cause in the *Essay on Criticism,* where his four specimens appear to restrict the phonetic expressiveness of verse to the categories of the loud-harsh, the smooth-soft, the slow, and the rapid. Yet it is not onomatopoeia exclusively or primarily which he is commending; in modern terminology, he wants to say that the meaning of a poem is inclusive of its sound as well as its paraphrasable statement. The 'echoes to the sense' either are rhythmical (accelerating or prolonging the line, interrupting it into staccato effect, or letting it flow in a legato) or they are phonative (euphonic or cacophonous—according to ease or difficulty of articulation); often these devices work together:

> Behold yon Isle, by Palmers, Pilgrims trod,
> *Men bearded, bald, cowled, uncowled, shod, unshod,*
> Peeled, patched, and pie-bald, linsey-woolsey brothers,
> Grave mummers! sleeveless some, and shirtless others.

Except for allowing himself the extra syllable in the feminine rhyme, Pope restricts himself to his decasyllabics; but though neoclassical doctrine allows for no further metrical variation than an occasional trochaic substitution, Pope's ear evades the rule by counting, as unstressed, syllables which any intelligent reading (including his own) must certainly have stressed, so permitting himself such a seven-stress line as has been cited. The excess of stressed syllables slows up the lines; the serried syntax gives an irregular, staccato movement; the dominance of plosives helps, with abruptness, in the total intended tone or 'meaning' of grotesqueness.

The neoclassical theory of serious diction called for a thinly honorific vocabulary, for adjectives which singled out an obvious attribute implicit in the noun—the "verdant" meadow, the "blue" violet—or were devised as loosely decorative epithets—the "pleasing" shades, the "grateful" clusters, the "fair" fields: all examples from the *Pastorals*. The inhibitions, imposed upon the joint authority of Philosophy and the Ancients, are stringent. Words must not be ambiguous or multiple-meaninged (for then they become puns, and puns are forms of verbal wit, and verbal wit is "false wit"); they must not be homely or technical (since poetry addresses men *as such*—gentlemen, not specialists in science or laborers); they must be lucid (for poetry owes its kinship with philosophy to its universality).

These inhibitions are removed or greatly mitigated, however, when the poet does not profess poetry but only an epistle or a burlesque imitation. The difference is notable in the *Moral Essays,* the *Rape,* the *Dunciad.*

> But hark! the chiming clocks to dinner call;
> A hundred footsteps *scrape* the Marble Hall;
> The rich buffet well-colored serpents grace,
> And *gaping* Tritons *spew* to wash your face.

> Whether the nymph shall break Diana's law,
> Or some frail China jar receive a flaw;
> Or stain her honor, or her new brocade;
> Forget her prayers, or miss a masquerade;
> Or lose her heart, or necklace, at a ball.

Zeugma, the joining of two unlike objects governed by a single verb, is of course a form of pun; yet this verbal play constitutes one of Pope's most poetic resources in the *Rape:* it is this device, one might say, which gives the tone to the whole.

Burlesque are both Pope's masterpieces, the *Rape* and the *Dunciad.* Of the mock-epic, we may provisionally say that it plays form against matter, a lofty and elaborate form against a trivial situation or set of persons or theme. But 'form against matter' is too simple a naming. The real failure of the post-Miltonic epic lay, surely, in the supposition that the heroic poem could be written in an unheroic age; that a poem which, generically, involved the interrelation of the human and the divine, the natural and the supernatural, could be written in an age when 'thinking people' had grown too prudent for heroism, too sophisticated for religion. John Dennis, whose taste among the Ancients was for Homer, Pindar, and Sophocles, and among the Moderns for Milton, was not unsound in his critical contention that great poetry like that of his favorites must be religious. So we might restate the incongruity as between heroic things and refined, between an age of faith and an age of reason. The mock-epic reminds an unheroic age of its own nature: by historical reference, it defines the 'civilized' present.

Is Pope, then, satirizing Belinda's world? Yes, but lightly. His intent is rather to juxtapose contrasting modes than to decide how far his aristocracy has gained by its elegance, how far lost by its safe distance from war, politics, poverty, and sin. The poem is in nothing more dexterous than in its controlled juxtaposition of worlds. In another context we should find ominous those brilliant lines which couple by incongruity the worlds of the bourgeoisie and the proletariat with that of the leisure class:

> The hungry Judges soon the sentence sign,
> And wretches hang that jury-men may dine;
> The merchant from the Exchange returns in peace,
> And the long labors of the Toilet cease.

The *Rape* owes its richness and resonance to its overstructure of powerful, dangerous motifs. What keeps it from being that filigree artifice which the romantics saw (and praised) is its playing with fire, especially the fires of sex and religion. Though Pope was scarcely a 'good Catholic,' his parents were devout; and he is writing of an 'old Catholic' society; and many of his effects involve the suggestion of blasphemous parallels: the linking of English folklore and the Lives of the Saints, and of both to his gentle mythology of urbane 'machines.' He links the nurse's moonlit elves and fairy ring with the priest's tales of "virgins visited by Angel-powers"; the visions of the Cave of Spleen are

> Dreadful as hermit's dreams in haunted shades,
> Or bright as visions of expiring maids,

visions which may or may not be reducible to physiological disturbances; the Baron and Belinda have their altars to Pride and Love, their real religions.

What, for religion, is got by parody parallel is, for sexual morality, managed by insinuation. Though it is admitted that nymphs may break Diana's law, we see none do so; the titular *Rape* is but of a lock. The opening of Canto III (a preview for the *School for Scandal*) shows the chorus at work ("At every word a reputation dies"); but we do not hear the death. A characteristic passage of *double-entendre* retails the difficulty of preserving a "melting maid's" purity at such a time and place of temptation as the midnight masquerade, while assuring us that her male companions' Honor, or her sylph, preserves her virtue.

Without doubt the specific perspectives through parody and irony are purposed. But there may be doubt whether these effects are not local and episodic, unsubject to central design and all-governing tone; for, though silly things have been said about Pope's work of composition (as if 'closed couplets' must all be equally discrete and unreconciled), he was, of course, so intent on making every verse exciting and finished as to make it difficult for the poem to subordinate them. In the case of the *Rape* he is often in danger but, I think, unvanquished. What organizes the poem is not exclusively the narrative, with its chronological and dramatic sequence of scenes (including two battles); it is yet more its tone—the steadiness with which it holds, against heroic and religious perspectives, to its seriocomic view of a little elegant society.

Not to the manor born, Pope makes the drawing-room seem an achievement. He so treats a woman's day, says Johnson, that "though nothing is disguised, everything is striking; and we feel all the appetite of curiosity for that from which we have a thousand times turned fastidiously away." Pope had not turned fastidiously away; like Proust, another 'outsider,' he was fascinated by the ritual which gave—or signified —the aristocratic status. He has practiced, on other matter, the Wordsworthian formula of giving to the unmarvelous the light of wonder. Society is a wonder, we are made to feel; convention a triumph of happy contrivance; coffee a luxury; a card game a crisis. This effect is in large measure the result of the 'machinery' of sylphs, who not only contrast with Homer's and Milton's 'machines' but parallel Pope's women—those coquettes, termagants, dociles, and prudes whose natures they abstract and stylize.

The burlesque of the *Rape* provides, then, an elaborate stratification of attitudes and effects: amusement at trifles taken seriously; delight at elegance; recollections of earlier literature (Homer and Spenser) in counterpoint against the current literary mode; juxtaposition of corresponding worlds (Achilles' shield, the great petticoat); reminders of the economic and political structures which make possible this leisure-class comedy, of the moral and religious structures which make possible a society at all.

In the *Dunciad,* the mock-heroic frame is intermittent. There are frequent local parodies of passages from Homer, Virgil, and Milton; there are classical devices like the Homeric games, the descent into the lower world, the preview of future history from the mount of vision; but there is no plot, no 'fable.' The loose organization is expressively loose. The poem tenders some recent episodes in a long contest between stupidity and intelligence, anarchy and culture, barbarism and civilization. In this long contest, stupidity and its allies win out, not because of their superior plans, designs, or purposes—for there is no real war of opposed strategies—but because of their sheer multitudinous mass, their dead weight. The poem, a kind of anti-masque, is a series of ritual tableaux and pageants and processions, chiefly sluggish of movement and visually dusky. There are occasional light reliefs, like the episode of the dilettanti, fresh from the grand tour, where (in lines which, for satiric effect, return to Pope's old Pastoral 'sweetness') one looks back

> To happy Convents, bosomed deep in vines,
> Where slumber Abbots, purple as their wines:
> To Isles of fragrance, lily-silvered vales,
> Diffusing languor in the panting gales.

But the general tone, prefigured in the brilliant Canto IV of the *Rape,* is somber and grotesque.

Time has assisted rather than damaged the poem. Though Pope's friends warned him against keeping alive his lampooned enemies, the warning was futile. Outside of literary circles, even in Pope's own time, most of the names must have been meaningless. And today it is certainly not the case that one need master footnotes to understand the poem Pope wrote; for the context provides the categories, which are permanent, while the proper names are annually replaceable. If one is confused by the blur of names, that too serves the purpose: these are not the names of the few masters but of the many applicants. As for the applicants: Pope is satirizing not bad men or poor men as such but bad poets and commercial publishers and undiscriminating patrons and pedantic professors. To relax one's critical standards is to be literarily immoral.

The finale is seriously epic because Pope credits the diabolical power of stupidity. In the myth of Book IV, civilization dies. According to Pope's view of history, brief episodes of enlightenment had all along alternated with far longer sequences of darkness: the primitive golden age gave way to barbarism; Roman civilization yielded to Gothic monkery and mummery; the Renaissance of Leo and Raphael and the Enlightenment of Newton and Locke and Bolingbroke were now threatened by extinction. What there is of the mythic and the dramatic in Pope comes from this sense. He felt the precariousness of civilization.

If this is a comic poem, it is comic only as *Volpone* is comic, by virtue of a grim extravagance, a grim grotesqueness; for it is not without reminder of the *Inferno* with its moral categories, its wry jokes, and its smoky lighting. The method involves not only "representative harmony" but visual imagery of a correspondent sort: the clumsiness and ugliness of the dull, the filthy foulness of their games, in which moral horror turns physical.

[50]

Slow rose a form, in majesty of Mud;
Shaking the horrors of his sable brows,
And each ferocious feature grim with ooze.

Pope was not a metaphysician; and it is unlikely that in another age he would have attempted to be, though he might well have been something else—a 'metaphysical poet.' His 'views' are flat and tiresome when he expresses them in general terms, when (as in his letters) he undertakes to moralize like a noble Roman. If he could turn a maxim, it was not this which made him, and keeps him, a poet but his power to see and hear what he felt, to find correlatives for his feelings toward people and doctrines. He images Hervey as a bug, a spaniel, a puppet, a toad; the scholars as grubs preserved in amber; the bad poet as a spider; the virtuosi as "locusts blackening all the land"; he sees Chaos regain its dominion.

Light dies before Thy uncreating word;
Thy hand, great Anarch! lets the curtain fall,
And Universal Darkness buries all.

1946

IV

GERARD MANLEY HOPKINS

THE early Hopkins follows Keats and the 'medieval school' (as he called the Pre-Raphaelites). The latest Hopkins, who wrote the sonnets of desolation, was a poet of tense, economic austerity. Their nearest parallel I can summon would be Donne's 'holy sonnets': "Batter my heart" and "If poisonous minerals." For the mode of "Andromeda" and the later sonnets (1885–89), Hopkins himself projected "a more Miltonic plainness and severity": He was thinking of Milton's sonnets and the choruses of *Samson*. In 1887 he invoked another name: "My style tends always more towards Dryden."

The middle period, which opens with the "Wreck of the Deutschland" (1885) and closes with "Tom's Garland" and "Harry Ploughman," both written in 1885, is the period of experiment. But it is also the most Hopkinsian—the most specially his own.

Middle Hopkins startles us by its dense rich world, its crowded Ark, its plenitude and its tangibility, its particularity of thing and word. There is detailed precision of image ("rose moles all in stipple upon trout that swim"). The poet is enamored of the unique, the "abrupt self."

The exploration of Middle Hopkins—its style, the view of life and art implicit in its style—may well start from the institutions and movements from which the poet learned, in which he participated. The motifs are the Ritualist Movement, Pre-Raphaelitism, Aestheticism, linguistic renovation, England, the Catholic church. In Hopkins' celebration of the sensuous, the concrete, the particular—his 'instress of the inscapes'—all of these converge.

As a Catholic, Hopkins was an incarnationist and a sacramentalist: the sacraments are the extensions of the Incarnation. As a Catholic he believed that man is a compound of matter and form and that his body, resurrected, will express and implement his soul through all eternity. "Man's spirit will be flesh-bound when found at best. But unencumbered. ...." Like all Catholic philosophers, he believed in an outer world independent of man's knowing mind—he was, in the present sense of the word, a "realist."

Hopkins was an Englishman, of a proud and patriotic sort. This is not always remembered, partly because he became the priest of a church viewed by other Englishmen as Continental, or Italian, or international. But there is an English way of being Catholic. Hopkins was not an 'old Catholic' of the sturdy, unemotional variety nourished on Challoner's *Garden of the Soul;* no convert could be that. But, like his admired Newman, and unlike Manning and Faber (also converts), he was 'Gallican,' not ultramontane; British, not Italian, in his devotional life and rhetoric. He remembers when England was Catholic, when the pilgrims frequented the shrine of Our Lady of Walsingham.

> Deeply surely I need to deplore it,
> Wondering why my master bore it,
>   The riving off that race
> So at home, time was, to his truth and grace

That a starlight-wender of ours would say
The marvellous Milk was Walsingham Way
And one—but let be, let be:
More, more than was will yet be.

The four real shapers of Hopkins' mind were all Britons;
we might go farther and say that all were British empiricists
—all concerned with defending the ordinary man's belief in
the reality and knowability of things and persons.

Two of them were encountered at Oxford. Pater, who remained his friend, was one of his tutors. Against the abstractions of the academic world, Pater boldly defended the concrete—in the visual arts and music, in perception. "Every
moment some form grows perfect in hand or face, some tone
on the hills or the sea is choicer than the rest....." Though
Hopkins could not conceivably have written so representa-
tively, abstractly ("hills....sea....choicer") the famous
Conclusion to *The Renaissance* pleads for a stressing of the
inscapes. Hopkins followed some lectures by Pater on Greek
philosophy; perhaps he heard, in an earlier version, Pater's
lectures on Plato and Platonism, in which, with monstrous
effrontery, the Doctrine of Ideas was praised as giving contex-
tual interest to the concrete.

With Ruskin, whose *Modern Painters* he read early and
admiringly, Hopkins revolted against the neoclassical grandeur of generality praised by Johnson and expounded by
Reynolds. The influence of Ruskin—art medievalist, devout
student of clouds, mountains, trees—is pervasive in Hopkins' sketches (five of which are reproduced in the *Note-
Books*) and in his journalizing, his meticulously technical
descriptions of church architecture (often neo-Gothic) and
scenery.

Hopkins follows the general line of Ruskin in more than art. He does not find the humanly satisfactory and well-furnished world such an effect of its Creator as the watch of the watchmaker. Nor does he, after the fashion of some mystics and Alexandrians, dissolve Nature into a system of symbols translating the real world of the Spirit. Like Ruskin, he was able to recover the medieval and Franciscan joy in God's creation. And, like Ruskin, he protested against an England which is "seared with trade.... and wears man's smudge." His political economy, as well as it can be construed, was Ruskinian—what may be called tory socialist or distributist.

It was to Newman, his great predecessor, that Hopkins wrote upon deciding to become a Roman Catholic. And Newman's closest approach to a philosophical work, his *Grammar of Assent* (1870), interested Hopkins enough so that in 1883 he planned to publish (had Newman agreed) a commentary on it. There were marked temperamental and intellectual differences between the men. Newman, much the more complex and psychologically subtle, could feel his way into other men's minds as Hopkins could not. Hopkins was the closer dialectician and scholar. He did not share Newman's distrust of metaphysics (including the scholastic), his tendency to fideism; but he was, like Newman—in words the latter used of Hurrell Froude—"an Englishman to the backbone in his severe adherence to the real and the concrete."

The great medieval thinker who most swayed Hopkins' spirit to peace, Duns Scotus, was also a Briton, had been an Oxford professor. He was "of reality the rarest-veinéd unraveler": he was able to analyze, disengage from the complex in which they appear, the thinnest, most delicate strands ('vein' may be either anatomical or geological). Perhaps "rarest-veinéd unraveler" is a kind of kenning for the philosopher's epithet, the Subtle Doctor. Scotus, the Franciscan critic of the Dominican Aquinas, was centrally dear to Hopkins as undertaking the philosophical validation of the individual. In the individual's relation to his species, Aquinas taught that the 'matter' individuates, while the 'form' is generic: that is, that the individuals of a species reproductively multiply their common originative pattern. Scotus insisted that each individual has a distinctive 'form' as well: a *haecceitas,* or thisness, as well as a generic *quidditas,* or whatness.

After having discovered this medieval Franciscan, Hopkins, upon "any inscape of sky or sea," thought of Scotus. The word, of Hopkins' coinage, occurs already in his Oxford notebooks. Modeled presumably on 'landscape,' 'inscape' stands for any kind of formed or focused view, any pattern discerned in the natural world. A central word in his vocabulary and central motif in his mental life, it traverses some range of meaning: from sense-perceived pattern to inner form. The prefix seems to imply a contrary, an outerscape: that is, an 'inscape' is not mechanically or inertly present but requires personal action, attention, a seeing and a seeing into.

The earliest "Notes for Poetry" cite: "Feathery rows of young corn. Ruddy, furred and branchy tops of the elms backed by rolling clouds." "A beautiful instance of inscape *sided* on the *slide,* that is successive sidings on one inscape, is seen in the behavior of the flag flower." In 1873, two years before the "Deutschland," he "saw a shoal of salmon in the river and many hares on the open hills. Under a stone hedge was a dying ram: there ran slowly from his nostrils a thick flesh-coloured ooze, scarlet in places, coiling and roping its way down so thick that it looked like fat."

He made notes on ancient musical instruments and on gems and their colors: "beryl—watery green; carnelian—strong flesh red, Indian red....." His love of precise visual observation never lapsed, nor did his taste for research. Like Gray, he had a meticulous antiquarianism, suited to botany or archeology, to notes and queries, details, studies in place names, amateur etymologies.

Perhaps his most brilliant prose celebrates the Self and its wonders: "That taste of myself, of I and me above and in all things, which is more distinctive than the taste of ale or alum." Other selves were mysterious. As a shy man, he found it easier to reach natural 'inscapes.' He wrote no psychological portraits matching for sharpness and delicacy his notations of ash trees. The men in his poems are seen as from a distance —sympathetically but generically.

But he gloried in the range and repertory of mankind. Chesterton was concerned that, lying down with the lamb, the lion should "still retain his royal ferocity"; and Hopkins, also, wanted monks to be mild and soldiers to be pugnacious. He imagined Christ incarnate again as a soldier. He didn't want other men to be like himself; he was drawn to his anti-types—to soldiers; miners; Felix Randall, the blacksmith, and Harry, the ploughman; to manual laborers. Moreover, each of these men he wished to be functioning not only characteristically but intensely, violently, dangerously—on their mettle, like the Windhover, like Harry Ploughman, like the sailor of the 'Eurydice' who, "strung by duty, is strained to beauty."

[57]

In poetry he desired both to record inscapes and to use words as objects. His was a double particularity.

Poetry, he wrote shortly before composing the "Deutschland," is "speech framed to be heard for its own sake and interest even over and above its interest of meaning. Some [subject] matter and meaning is essential to it but only as an element necessary to support and employ the shape which is contemplated for its own sake. Poetry is in fact speech for the inscape's sake—and therefore the inscape must be dwelt on."

In 1862 he was already collecting words. The earliest entries in the *Note-Books* are gritty, harshly tangy words, 'running the letter,': "grind, gride, grid, grit, groat, grate" and "crock, crank, kranke, crick, cranky." He collected dialectal equivalents: "whisket" for "basket," "grindlestone" for "grindstone." He notes linguistic habits: that an observed laborer, when he began to speak "quickly and descriptively,—dropped or slurred the article." He attends to, and tries to define, the sundry modes of Latin pronunciation. He inquires concerning the character of the Maltese language; wants to learn Welsh—not primarily in order to convert the local Wesleyans back to their ancestral faith.

In his early poetry Hopkins followed Keats and the 'medieval school.' Even in his middle style there remain vestiges of the earlier decorative diction, frequent use of "beauty," "lovely," "dear," "sweet" ("that sweet's sweeter ending"). But as early as 1866, "The Habit of Perfection," though dominantly 'medieval,' anticipates the later mode:

> This ruck and reel which you remark
> Coils, keeps, and teases simple sight.

"The Wreck of the Deutschland" (1875) inaugurates Hopkins' middle period (his first proper mastery). The diction is quite as extraordinary as the rhythm. Characteristic are homely dialectal words, sounding like survivors from Old English, and compound epithets suggestive of the same archetype. From the concluding stanzas of the "Deutschland" come these lines:

> Mid-numbered He in three of the thunder-throne!
> Not a dooms-day dazzle in his coming nor dark as he came....

and

> Dame, at our door
> Drowned, and among our shoals,
> Remember us in the roads, the heaven-haven of the
> Reward.....

From "The Bugler's First Communion":

> Forth Christ from cupboard fetched, how fain I of feet
> To his youngster take his treat!
> Low-latched in leaf-light housel his too huge godhead.

That Hopkins was influenced by Old English poetry is an easy assumption. In his excellent *New Poets from Old: A Study in Literary Genetics,* Henry Wells observes that all the technical features representative of that poetry appear conspicuously in Hopkins; judges him far nearer to Cynewulf than to Chaucer; and finds a plausible parallel to a passage in *Beowulf.* But, by his own statement, Hopkins did not learn Anglo-Saxon until 1882 and seems never to have read either *Beowulf* or Cynewulf. In any case, he was already a student of Welsh poetry and an attentive reader of linguistic monographs. Like Pound and Eliot, he belongs among the poets who can be incited to poetry by scholars' prose.

In 1873–74, while teaching a course in rhetoric at Manresa

House, Hopkins wrote the observations collected in the *Note-Books*. In his notes he used the 1859 *Lectures on the English Language* by the American scholar, George P. Marsh, a book calculated to incite a poet. Marsh has a real interest in the future (as well as the past) of the language and a real interest in the literary (as well as the pragmatic) use of words. The whole direction of his book suggests that literary experiment can find much to its purpose in literary history and that new poetry can be engendered by old. Ending his lecture on "Accentuation and Double Rhymes," he urges: "We must enlarge our stock [of rhyming words] by the revival of obsolete words and inflections from native sources," or introduce substitutes for rhyme; in the following chapter he excitingly discusses alliteration (with illustrations from *Piers Plowman*), consonance, e.g., 'bad, led'; 'find, band' (with illustrations from Icelandic poetry and invented English examples), and assonance (with illustrations from the Spanish). Hopkins' quotations from *Piers* are Marsh's; only in 1882 did he study *Piers,* and then without admiration, regarding its verse as a "degraded and doggerel" form of Anglo-Saxon sprung rhythm.

To both Bridges and Dixon, curious concerning the new poetic method of the "Deutschland," Hopkins says nothing of Old English or of *Piers Plowman* but speaks of nursery rhymes, the choruses of Milton's *Samson,* and his readings in Welsh poetry (which he began studying in 1875). "The chiming of the consonants I get in part from the Welsh, which is very rich in sound and imagery." Traits common to Old English and Middle Hopkins (scant use of articles, prepositions, and pronouns; constant use of compound words) are shared by both with Welsh poetry.

There is a third lineage for the diction of Hopkins. Through

Barnes and Furnivall, at least, he derives from an imprecisely defined group of Victorian historians and philologists, who challenged the dominance of the Latin and Romance—the 'civilized,' learned, abstract—elements in our language. One of these linguistic protestants was the Oxford historian, E. A. Freeman, who chronicled the Norman Conquest and himself resisted it. As early as 1846 he was praising the Teutonic part of our language as affording "expressions mostly of greater strength than their Romance synonyms for all purposes of general literature"; and he used the phrase "pure English" for a diction purged of these synonyms. Another Anglicizer was F. J. Furnivall, a founder, in 1864, of the Early English Text Society, and a constant editor of texts, who began his intellectual career under the influence of Ruskin and Maurice and declared that his interest in early literature was not linguistic but social. Another founder of the E.E.T.S., R. C. Trench, gave a chapter of his *English, Past and Present* (1855) to a consideration of "English as it might have been" without a Norman Conquest. Though our present cerebral and technical words derive from the classical languages, he argues that the Anglo-Saxon might have developed—chiefly by compounding, as German has done—such a vocabulary. Even "impenetrability" could have been matched, accurately, by "unthoroughfaresomeness." And theological language would be understood by farm hand as well as by scholar if we said "again-buying" for "redemption."

In the tradition of Trench, but much more violent, William Barnes lamented the linguistic conquest of English and declared the old stock still capable of extension by compounding. Instead of "photograph," we should say "sunprint" or "flameprint." Indeed, all our current Latinisms we should replace out of the "wordstores of the landfolk." Barnes's nominations are all flavorsome; samples are "overyearn" (commiserate), "gleecraft" (music), "outclear" (elucidate), "faithheat" (enthusiasm). He regretted the loss of "inwit" in place of "conscience"; and to serve instead of "subjective" and "objective" (those psychological-philosophical terms which Coleridge introduced from Germany) he suggested "inwoning" and "outwoning."

Barnes had something of a following among literary people; was publicly praised by Patmore, Gosse, Bridges, Hardy. His poetry, early read, Hopkins preferred to that of Burns, liking its "West Country instress." But he learned most from the prose. Barnes's *Speechcraft* [i.e., Grammar], says Hopkins, is "written in an unknown tongue, a soul of modern Anglo-Saxon, beyond all that Furnival in his wildest Forewords ever dreamed..... It makes one weep to think what English might have been, for in spite of all that Shakespeare and Milton have done with the compound ['impure' English] I cannot doubt that no beauty in a language can make up for want of purity. In fact, I am learning Anglo-Saxon and it is a vastly superior thing to what we have." He cites Barnes's wondrous "pitches of suchness" (for 'degrees of comparison'): "We *ought* to call them so, but alas!"

Hopkins' characteristic critical and philosophical terminology follows closely the counsel of Trench and Barnes: that is, it is a compounding of Old English roots and suffixes to suit new needs and to replace Latinic terms. "Inwit" (for "conscience") and Barnes's "inwoning" (subjective) may have suggested "instress" and "inscape." Hopkins explains his special use of "sake" (the being a thing has outside itself) by analytic parallel of the compounds "forsake," "namesake," "keepsake." The terminology of the *Comments on the Spiritual Exercises* (1880) is particularly Hopkinsian (e.g., "pitch," "stress," "burl"). To Bridges, Hopkins wrote of his manuscript book on rhythm, "It is full of new words, without which there can be no new science."

His doctrine of the language for poetry, nowhere exposited, we can infer to have been quite different. Archaism—the use of obsolete words for literary effect—he repudiated. His oddities (like "pashed," "fashed," "tucked," "degged") are generally dialectal; and it is safe to assume that his words of Old English lineage were collected and used by him as dialectal, still-spoken English: not 'inkhorn' terms but folk speech. Even when he thought he was improvising, he was—at least in one instance—remembering: his alleged coinage, 'louched' (slouched, slouching) was, as Bridges observed, to be found in Wright's Dialect Dictionary.

Whenever Hopkins explained his words (as he always stood ready to do), their particularity, their compactness and detail, were manifest. "Stickles—Devonshire for the foamy tongues of water below falls." "Bole" is not only used by poets but seems technical and proper and in the mouth of timber merchants and so forth. Of "flit," questioned by a correspondent, he writes: "I myself always use it and commonly hear it used among our people. I think it is at least a North Country word, used in Lancashire, for instance."

His compoundings are another matter. Though analogues can be offered from Browning, Hopkins came to them, it is probable, by way of medieval poetry, English and Welsh, and by way of Marsh, Trench, and Barnes. His defense would doubtless be that to compound freely was to restore to the English language a power it once had possessed. But the words thus compounded, or the root and suffix or prefix, were separately familiar and oral. He writes "spend-savour salt" (the salt which is spending its savor and on its way to being the biblical salt which has lost its savor); "bloomfall"; "tram-beam"; "backwheels"; "though worlds of *wanwood leafmeal lie*" ("leafmeal" is on the model of "piecemeal"; suffix means "by bits," "by portions").

Judged by its effect and its internal intent, Hopkins' poetry finds partial parallels in Holst, Delius, and Vaughan Williams. Avoiding the archaism of Warlock and Dolmetsch, they sought to resume the line of English music where its genuine succession was interrupted—at the Restoration, and to go creatively back to the English glory of folksong and madrigal and the modal scales, to Dowland, Bull, and Byrd. Similarly, Hopkins seems to be reaching back, while he is reaching forward, to an 'English' poetry. Probably, we may add, to an 'English Catholic' poetry; and suppose that his pushing back of the Elizabethans had some incentive in his desire to get back of the Reformation to an England at once Catholic and English.

Like the poetry of the bards and the scops, Hopkins' poetry is oral, yet not conversational but formal and rhetorical. It uses dialectal words without intending, like Barnes's *Poems of Rural Life,* to be local and homely; it uses folk words in 'serious' poetry. Hopkins' poems were written for an ideal audience, never existent in his day or ours, composed of literarily perceptive countrymen and of linguistically adept and folk-minded scholars. What his poetry assumed as convention, he had, by artifice, to create. "The Wreck" and "Tom's Garland" suggest or predict a greater poetry than they achieve. Hopkins' experiments are yet more important than his achievement; his comparative failures more interesting than his good 'whole poems.'

The ideal of poetry must be to instress the inscapes without splintering the architecture of the universe and, expressionally, to make every word rich in a way compatible with a more than additively rich total poetic structure. But in Hopkins' poems, the word, the phrase, the "local excitement," often pulls us away from the poem. And in the more ambitious pieces, the odes as we may call them ("The Wreck," "Spelt from Sibyl's Leaves," "Nature Is a Heraclitean Fire"), there is felt a discrepancy between texture and structure: the copious, violent detail is matched by no corresponding intellectual or mythic vigor. Indeed, "The Wreck of the Deutschland" is an 'occasional,' commissioned piece at which Hopkins works devotedly and craftfully, like Dryden at his *Annus mirabilis,* but which, like Dryden's poem, falls apart. Hopkins was not a story-teller, and he was not able to turn his wrecks into myths of wreck; they remain historical events accompanied by commentary. "The Bugler-Boy" and other poems suffer from the gap between the psychological naïveté and the purely literary richness. To try prose paraphrases of the middle poems is invariably to show how thin the 'thinking' is. Hopkins' mind was first aesthetic and then technical: he reasoned closely upon metaphysical and prosodic matters. But his reflections upon beauty, man, and nature—his humanistic thoughts—are not distinguished.

The meaning of Hopkins' poems hovers closely over the text, the linguistic surface. The rewarding experience of concern with them is to be let more and more into words and their ways, to contemplate the protopoetry of derivation and metaphorical expansion, to stress the inscapes of the English tongue.

1944

V

WILLIAM BUTLER YEATS
THE RELIGION OF A POET

YEATS needed religion less as a man than as a poet, and his need was epistemological and metaphysical: he needed to believe that poetry is a form of knowledge and power, not of amusement. One might say of the early Yeats that he thought of poetry as incantation and meant the word as more than metaphor; of the later Yeats, one would have to say that his metaphors were meant as more than illustrative analogies. Of symbolism, the juncture between religion and poetry, he could never have admitted its "mereness": symbols are vehicles as well as intimations. If mathematical and chemical formulas are recipes for the control of matter, images and liturgy have power over minds; they reach farther and deeper than do abstractions. Men become what they contemplate.

The last decades of the nineteenth century did not lack the sense, now become more ominous, of being at the "end of our time." Men were asking, practically—not as ritual prelude to catechetical instruction—whether life was worth living. They were doubting the gain of improved instrumentalities. Unable to hold their old faith, they were unable to relinquish it and were tormented by their indecision. "Seigneur, prenez pitié du chrétien qui doute, de l'incrédule qui voudrait croire." Des Esseintes's melodramatic cry, muted, can be heard in the suave, sad pages of *Marius*. Frederick Myers writes, in 1900, of "the deep disquiet of our time..... On the one hand, health, intelligence, morality,—all such boons as the steady progress of planetary evolution can win for man,— are being achieved in increasing measure. On the other hand, this very sanity, this very prosperity, do but bring out in stronger relief the underlying *Weltschmerz,* the decline of any real belief in the dignity, the meaning, the endlessness of life."

Young Yeats read Darwin and Huxley and accepted them as "established authority." But upon consideration he saw that their beliefs contravened his imagination; and he could not accept as doctrines their assumptions and methods. While others lauded "progress," he turned to that kind of tradition-ary primitivism which supposes central insights into human nature to occur more easily at the beginning of a culture than at the end of a civilization. Like A.E. he was not a university man; he had indeed a prejudice against meek readers in libraries; and—by reaction as well as chance, doubtless—he sought out first the unprofessional books professing to teach wisdom of life. In search of a philosophy "at once logical and boundless" he read Baron Reichenbach on Odic Force, Boehme, Swedenborg. An "authoritative religion," he de-cided, could be assembled from the affirmations of the poets— especially Spenser, Blake, and Shelley.

His emancipated father took no stock in religion; and it was this parental unbelief which forced the son to examine the arguments and evidences with care. "I weighed this mat-ter perpetually with great anxiety, for I did not think I could live without religion." Much later, writing of his occult studies, he protests that he has not taken them up "wilfully nor through love of strangeness nor love of excitement.... but because unaccountable things had happened even in my childhood and because of an ungovernable craving."

The grandparents were Anglicans of the Evangelical persuasion; and they took the child to church, where he found pleasure in the hymns, the sermon, and the poetry of Ecclesiastes and the Apocalypse—predictable tastes. In later life he occasionally visited Anglican churches; but, as an Irish boy in a London school, under a clerical headmaster "as temperate in his religious life as in all else," he had been repelled by the ease with which English religion passed into respectability. Nor could the moderations and negations of the altarless Church of Ireland be expected to attract the devotion of a young man in search of symbolism and audacity. And "Protestant Ireland seemed to think of nothing but getting on in the world."

Despite his close friendships with Dowson and Lionel Johnson and his subsequent association with Baron von Hügel, Yeats never seriously considered becoming a Catholic. Though impressed by the neo-Catholic movement among the young French intellectuals (Claudel, Péguy, Psichari), he was also puzzled: such concern for the church as he had known in the nineties was the concern of Barbey d'Aurevilly and Huysmans—Catholics with a taste for magic, sadism, or Satanism. To be sure, Celtic Ireland is also Catholic. But in *Ireland's Literary Renaissance* (1916), Ernest Boyd, who can cite only Katherine Tynan as a Catholic writer, remarks the Irish impossibility of *grands convertis* like Huysmans or

Verlaine. The "Protestantism of the Irish Catholic is such as to deprive the Church of precisely those elements which are favourable to literary and intellectual development, and have rallied so many artists to her support." If the Church of Ireland is very Protestant, so, and in another sense, is the Catholic church in Ireland. And so, to find a faith really suited to the Irish genius, the 'Dublin mystics' (as Boyd calls Eglinton and A.E.) adopted the ancient Irish pantheon, the *Tuatha De Danann,* and the *sidhe.* With his friends, Yeats turned from St. Patrick (whether Catholic or Anglican) to Oisin and Niamh and Aengus. He began to chart the Sacred Mountains of Ireland on his map, to wander about raths and fairy hills, to question old peasants; he longed to be carried away by the fairies; he found beneath the Catholic stratum more primitive deposits of faith. A countrywoman told him that she disbelieved in ghosts and hell—the latter, an invention of priests for their own profit; "but there are fairies," she hastened to supplement, "and little leprechauns, and water-horses and fallen angels": Whatever else one doubts, one never doubts the fairies, for—as another peasant said to the same inquirer, "They stand to reason."

Thus encouraged, Yeats rejected Christian authority. There must, he maintains, be a "tradition of belief older than that of any European Church, and founded upon the experience of the world before the modern bias." He writes to a French friend: "I have not found my tradition in the Catholic Church, which was not the church of my childhood, but where the tradition is, as I believe, more universal and more ancient." And to this position he persuaded Lady Gregory. "I have longed to turn Catholic that I might be nearer to the

[69]

people," she testified; "but you have taught me that paganism brings me nearer still."

Of course Yeats pointed out to Lady Gregory that neither she nor her peasants were pure pagans; and in earlier days he did not oppose such a properly contaminated Christianity as a peasant might practice or an esoteric Christian speculatively construct. Both *The Celtic Twilight* (1893) and *The Secret Rose* (1896) use thematically the interplays—the rivalries and interpenetrations—of the Christian and the pagan. In "The Crucifixion of the Outcast," the White Friars put to death a pagan gleeman because his mythic songs, so different from those of their own pious poets, arouse "forgotten longing in their hearts." But when, in another story, Puritan troopers break down the door of the abbey and shoot the White Friars at the altar, and the abbot, crucifix high over his head, condemns the profaners to dwell among the ungovernable shadows, it is the Gaelic deities who lead them to destruction. One and the same "happy theologian" has visions of Christ and of the people of fairy.

Yeats himself early became a pagan. Reading *Walden,* he was inspired to conquer bodily desire and become a hermit: living "as Thoreau lived, seeking wisdom"; it was this desire for the ascetic's solitude which he commemorated in the early popular lyric, "The Lake Isle of Innisfree." Recurrent for him, throughout his life, is the image of Milton's hermetic scholar.

> Or let my lamp at midnight hour
> Be seen in some high lonely tower,
> Where I may oft outwatch the *Bear*
> With Thrice-Great Hermes, or unsphere
> The spirit of Plato. . . . .

But such desire for solitude and lonely contemplation is less characteristic of his confessedly gregarious spirit than a series of entries into esoteric cults, communion of adepts.

In 1885, when he was twenty, he met with A. P. Sinnett's *Esoteric Buddhism,* a chief scripture of the Theosophical movement; he interested his friend, Charles Johnson, who founded the Hermetic Society, soon renamed the Dublin Lodge of the Theosophical Society. In London, shortly after, Yeats nightly frequented the establishment of Theosophy's discoverer and founder, Mme Helena Blavatsky. The Society for Psychical Research had just finished its scrutiny of the Theosophical revelations; it had pronounced them fraudulent, and the movement had dwindled. But Yeats felt an instinctive admiration, not subsequently renounced, for this "sort of old Irish peasant woman with an air of humour and audacious power," this "great passionate nature, a sort of female Dr. Johnson, impressive . . . . to every man or woman who had themselves any richness." One night a week she answered questions on her system, was calm and philosophic; on other evenings she was busy, shrewd, racily humorous— played patience, reckoning her score on the green baize table top while cranks "from half Europe and from all America" talked into her imperturbable ears.

Esoteric Buddhism, Yeats's introduction to Theosophy, purports to publish the secret teaching of spiritual adepts living in the remotest Himalayas. As a movement, Theosophy offers itself as an interpretation of the inner meaning of world religion, Christian as well as Buddhist; it attaches much historical importance to Alexandrian Neo-Platonism, both pagan and Christian, as its ancestor; it has developed, historically, from the spiritualist movement; it is sympathetic in its attitude toward astrology, alchemy, and such. Like pure Buddhism, Theosophy has no God, and consequently no atonement and no prayer. It teaches the Hindu and Buddhist doctrine of karma: that our rewards or punishments in future incarnations proceed, as by natural law, from our characters in the last. Like Buddhism, it exhorts to the destruction of desire and anticipates the eventual release from the wheel of existence and entrance into nirvana.

At the British Museum, Yeats encountered S. L. Mac-Gregor Mathers, Bergson's brother-in-law. Mathers, who had assisted Mme Blavatsky in her *Secret Doctrine* and translated *The Kabbalah Unveiled,* founded, at London, the Iris-Urania Temple of the Hermetic Students of the Golden Dawn, an order which professed to derive its rituals from old Rosicrucian manuscripts. Yeats was initiated into the order in its first year, 1887; and Mathers had a long, deep, and acknowledged influence over him. In "All Souls Night" of 1920, Yeats remembers his adept:

> I call up MacGregor from the grave....
> He had much industry at setting out,
> Much boisterous courage, before loneliness
> Had driven him crazed;
> For meditations upon unknown thought
> Make human intercourse grow less and less.....

It was presumably Mathers who introduced Yeats to the "Christian Cabbala"—a name loosely given to writings of the sixteenth and seventeenth centuries, notably those of Pico della Mirandola, Reuchlin, Cornelius Agrippa, Henry More, and *The Kabbala Denudata* of Rosenroth.[1] Yeats fre-

1. Cf. J. L. Blau, *The Christian Interpretation of the Cabala in the Renaissance* (New York, 1944). For Mather's Order and its contexts, cf. A. E. Waite, *Brotherhood of the Rosy Cross* (London, 1924); and Alvin B. Kuhn, *Theosophy....* (New York, 1930).

quently cites Agrippa's *De occulta philosophia,* a work which has much to say of magic and magical images and astrology and the World Soul. According to Agrippa, all terrestrial things owe their power to their celestial patterns; and by a proper knowledge of their correspondences we may use the earthly images to induce the occult powers. Each sign of the zodiac, each face of each sign, each planet, has its image; and these images imprinted in seals and rings, made at proper times and of proper materials, can effect these powers; so, too, can images not celestial which are made at the astrologically proper times: thus, to procure love one devises figures embracing one another; to bring about disaster, one breaks an image.

Under Mathers' instruction, Yeats learned how to paint cabalistic symbols on cards and how to use them for evoking states of reverie in himself and sometimes trance states in others. Yeats tells some extraordinary stories of these experiments; but at the end of "Hodos chameliontos," he passes a judgment of rejection, not denying power to the symbols chosen but perceiving that irresponsible play with them brings danger. The images that really matter to men of genius and culture are the images which are not chosen but given; and the unity of a culture comes from a given image— the figure of Apollo or of Christ.

In Paris at the end of the century, Yeats scrutinized the chief occultists. With the followers of the eighteenth-century mystic, Saint-Martin, he tested the vision-producing potency of hashish. He met a young Arabic scholar possessing a ring of alchemical gold. He visited the "mysterious house" of Marquis Stanislas de Guaita, founder (in 1889) of the Ordre Kabbalistique de la Rose-Croix and author of *La Clef de la magie noire* and *Le Serpent de la Genèse;* admired the Mar-

[73]

quis as "the one eloquent learned scholar who has written of magic in our generation." He met also the great Sar Péladan, founder (in 1890) of yet another, a professedly Catholic, order of the Rosy Cross. Péladan, described by Max Nordau in his once famous *Degeneration,* claimed to be the descendant of the old Magi, the inheritor of the arcane wisdom of Zoroaster, Pythagoras, and Orpheus; and his order purported to revive and unite with the Rosicrucians the Knights Templars and the order of the Holy Grail. The Rosicrucians, professing to reconcile Christianity with Cabalism, provided Yeats with his obsessive symbol of the rose—especially the "Rose upon the Rood of Time" (1893); and in his essay of 1895, "The Body of the Father Christian Rosencrux," he symbolizes an old myth of the order, according to which, two hundred and fifty years after the founder's death, his disciples found in a sealed temple his imperishable body.

In "Hodos chameliontos," Yeats confesses that he had himself ambitions of becoming founder of a "mystical order" which should buy or hire a castle in Lough Kay, a castle affording at one end "a stone platform where meditative persons might pace to and fro." This castle on the rock would provide a place "where its members could retire for a while for contemplation, and establish mysteries like those of Eleusis and Samothrace." For ten years (1888–98?) he sought "to find philosophy and create ritual for the Order." Perhaps, as for Boehme, Swedenborg, and Blake, so again the gates of revelation would open; and he was prepared that the new scripture should, like that of the great mystics whom he had read, use Christian symbols as well as pagan. "Is it true that our air is disturbed, as Mallarmé said, by 'the trembling of the veil of the temple, or that our whole age is seeking to bring forth a sacred book?' Some of us thought that book near towards the end of last century, but the tide sank again."

Acquaintance with Theosophists, Cabalists, and Rosicrucians lay behind Yeats's endeavor to write a novel, the hero of which should "see all the modern visionary sects pass before his bewildered eyes, as Flaubert's St. Anthony saw the Christian sects." This abandoned manuscript of 1896, which must have owed much to Pater as well as to Flaubert, may well be represented by the three tales, "Rosa Alchemica," "The Magi," and "The Tables of the Law," published in 1897 and introducing the figures of Michael Robartes and Owen Aherne, the adepts who reappear in "The Phases of the Moon" and elsewhere. Told in the elaborate, thick harmonies of the *Imaginary Portraits,* these stories summon up adepts in risk of losing their sanity as they have already lost their taste for human intercourse, even for intercourse with other students—men like Pater's Van Storck, like Huysmans's Des Esseintes, like Villier's Axel. The narrator is a reformed adept, now a Catholic, who, though conscious of the malign in esoteric cults, has but half suppressed his desire for the dangerous, for that "indefinite world" which invites the soul to waver, wander, and perish. While professing renunciation, the vain soul still hovers over her former state, proud to have sinned. The other tales offer the same image of the divided soul. In the second, Owen Aherne has grown wise to his own damnation. It has been revealed to him that only through sin and separation from God can he come to God; but he cannot sin, he cannot pray. "I have seen the Whole," he says, "and how can I come again to belief that a part is the whole?" In the third tale, concerned with the return of the Magi and the beginning of a new cycle, a Second Coming, the teller speaks of dreading the illusions which accompany any age of revelation; and he concludes: "I no longer live an elaborate and haughty life, but seek to lose myself among the prayers and the sorrows of the multitude. I pray best in poor chapels, where the frieze coats brush past me as I kneel, and when I pray against demons....." Despite their perioded style, these pieces have their power and horror—a horror drawn not from blasphemy or diabolism but from the fear of madness.

All the cults to which Yeats attached himself vary a single pattern—that of an arcane wisdom traditionally clothed in myth but now, to some group of initiates, "unveiled"; all of them—even theosophy, the most elaborate of the systems—are inclusive of magic, alchemy, astrology, and spiritualism. These concerns of Yeats are all defined and defended by Mme Blavatsky, who devoted the first volume of her *Isis Unveiled* to magic, past and present; who asserted that "astrology is to exact astronomy what psychology is to exact physiology"; and who pointed out that, under the emblems of sulphur, mercury, and salt, alchemy may concern itself with human and cosmic mysteries.

Yeats played with alchemy and its symbolisms. He imagined himself as writing a little work, in the style of Sir Thomas Browne, which should interpret the alchemic quest as the "transmutation of life into art." He learned to cast horoscopes; in the Preface to his early novel, *John Sherman,* he writes: "I am something of an astrologer, and can see" in these pages a young man "born when the Water-Carrier Aquarius was on the horizon, at pains to overcome Saturn in Saturn's hour, just as I can see in much that follows his

[76]

struggle with the still all-too-unconquered Moon, and at last, as I think, the summons of the prouder Sun." Technical terms of the 'science' are not infrequent in *A Vision;* more significant, however, is the general analogy between the "Twenty-eight Incarnations" and the structure of a popular manual like Evangeline Adams' *Astrology* (1927). Both offer sequences of characterological types, illustrated from the biography of genius; both offer shrewd, suggestive analyses of types and individuals. But, unlike Miss Adams, Yeats is not offering a literal equation of celestial influences and terrestrial products; he professes that the fitting of the lunar series into the solar year is purely arbitrary and that the whole series is a "parable." In a fashion for which astrologers offer no authority, he orders his types so that they constitute a gradual progression from the most objective to the most subjective and back again; and he combines a psychology with a history by making the same diagram serve at once for a vertical view of two thousand years (the Great Wheel, comprising twenty-eight successive incarnations) and a horizontal view of all types contemporarily occurrent.

His degree of faith in the predictive power of horoscopes is difficult to estimate; but it is not difficult to conjecture the imaginative and philosophical value which the 'science' held for him: it lay in the honorific connection astrology establishes between man and nature and in its imprecise determinism of the individual and the state.

One must be at least equally cautious in estimating Yeats's attitude toward spiritualism, apparently the latest to develop of his occult interests. He was critical of alleged communications with the dead and the interpretation of the 'messages.' He did not forget the warnings of Swedenborg (whose *Heaven and Hell* he read in his youth) that the spirits who can reach men through mediums are either earth-bound or devils counterfeiting the virtuous dead. In his discourse prefatory to "The Words upon the Window-Pane," he argues that every manifestation of a spirit is "first of all a secondary personality or dramatisation created by, in, or through the medium." He even suggests, though he but half accepts his suggestion, the theory that the communicators of *A Vision* were not spirits of the dead but the "personalities of a dream" shared by his wife and him; the test of truth for him lies certainly not in the mode of its delivery but in its coherence and illumination. For the credulous "millions who have substituted the séance-room for the church" he had only pity and contempt.

Whatever the precise nature of his interest in spiritualism, it had little to do with curiosity concerning man's post-mortem existence and much to do with possible unseen worlds surrounding man now. In his *Human Personality* (1903), a book admired by William James and A.E. and surely known to Yeats, Myers discovers the cure for man's "spiritual solitude" in the law of telepathy, defined as the transference of ideas and images from living brain to living brain and as communion between incarnate and discarnate spirits. From the painful sense of the self's isolation, Yeats turned to the doctrine that beneath our conscious selves there is a communal psyche, an *Anima mundi.* The sharing of the same dream by two living persons and the invasion of the living man's dream by the dead man's memories are beliefs interconnected in Yeats's faith: they are parts of the same release from the uniqueness of the self.

How far Yeats believed in these mysterious worlds and

powers is a question to which his critics have long addressed themselves. The answer has often been skeptical. Before the publication of *A Vision,* Yeats was customarily, in contrast to A.E., viewed as one who toyed with mysticism, used it for literary effect. And certainly *The Celtic Twilight* (1893) is full of hints that Yeats is being romantic and misty and that the real Yeats is the shrewd observer who says of "A Visionary" (clearly A.E.) that there is in him "the vast and vague extravagance that lies at the bottom of the Celtic heart." But there are intimations of another attitude, hints of a Pyrrhonism which finds dreams as credible as facts, of a fideism which is not disturbed by the current and changing 'truths' of science. "Everything exists, everything is true" is one fashion of putting this; another is to ask, rhetorically, "When all is said and done, how do we not know but that our own unreason may be better than another's truth?"

Autobiographically considering his earlier self, Yeats suggests the Pascalian antithesis between the reasons of the head and the reasons of the heart: "My critical mind—was it friend or enemy?—mocked, and yet I was delighted." And of his youthful talks with peasants: "I did not believe with my intellect that you could be carried away body and soul, but I believed with my emotions, and the belief of the country people made that easy." But when he conversed with educated people he grew timid: "I was always ready to deny or turn into a joke what was for all that my secret fanaticism. When I had read Darwin and Huxley and believed as they did, I wanted, because an established authority was upon my side, to argue with everybody." Even in *A Vision* Yeats leaves room for the reader to think that he is being offered prose commentary on the symbolism of the poems.

Yet, if the earlier Yeats is whimsical or otherwise evasive on the subject of the occult, the later Yeats has cut himself off from such ambiguity. With whatever hesitations, cautions, and reserves, he ranges himself on the side of the supernaturalists. Responsibility of belief markedly increases from *The Celtic Twilight* to *A Vision*. In the Preface to the 1902 edition of the former, he announced, "I shall publish in a little while a big book about the commonwealth of faery, and shall try to make it systematic and learned enough to buy pardon for this handful of dreams." This announcement, which his critics took as further whimsy, indicates rather that Yeats was unsatisfied to leave his convictions in the twilight of poetic prose, that intellectual integrity required him to produce some philosophical defense of his convictions. The essays called "Magic" (1901) and "Per amica silentia lunae" (1917) represent preliminary efforts at such defense; but it is *A Vision* which, incorporating and developing the earlier ideas of the *Anima mundi,* of the self and its antithetic mask, especially fulfils the intention of 1902. "Learned" and "systematic" are relative terms, of course; but they can stand as descriptive of the intention toward which Yeats moved.

Until comparatively late, he had restricted his reading to the 'poets and the mystics,' avoided the philosophers, even the philosophers of mysticism—as though the purity of his intuitive belief might be violated by acquaintance with rival positions and criteria. But now, after making the initial notes for *A Vision,* he reads Plotinus, medieval philosophy, Berkeley, Hegel, Wundt, McTaggart, willing not only to see his own 'philosophy' in terms of its historical parallels and oppositions but to make it as coherent as possible; and he reads

biography and especially history with the intent of grounding
his myth in the world of secular fact. This movement from
the Rosicrucians to Plotinus and Berkeley is strikingly paralleled by the increasing comprehensiveness of Yeats's mythic
Ireland. Whereas in the *Twilight* and the *Rose* he almost
limits himself to the lore of peasants and the "pride of the
adept," to a pre-Christian, or, failing that, a pre-Reformation,
Ireland, the later Yeats is able to find heroes in the persons
of the Anglo-Irish Augustans—Swift, Burke, Goldsmith, and
Berkeley—and to find Irish philosophy in their writings.

> And haughtier-headed Burke that proved the State a tree,
> That this unconquerable labyrinth of the birds, century
> > after century,
> Cast but dead leaves to mathematical equality;
> And God-appointed Berkeley that proved all things a dream,
> That this pragmatical, preposterous pig of a world,
> > its farrow that so solid seem
> Must vanish on the instant if the mind but change its theme.....

Yeats's early traffic with ghosts, sorcerers, and fairies was,
probably, instigated by a desire to loosen the bonds of logic.
In his essay on "Demonology" Emerson speaks of the great
interest which dreams, animal magnetism, and omens have
for "some minds. They run into this twilight and say, 'There's
more here than is dreamed of in your philosophy.'" Young
Yeats was surely one of these 'minds'; he desired to say: Life
is not all rule, order, reason, system, common sense; nature
and the human mind have their 'night-side' of the subconscious, of dusk and half-lights. Religion he saw as the search
for the irrational, the irruptive, the unpredictable. But, without exaggerating the antithesis, one may represent the later
Yeats as finding its own logic and order in the supernatural.

[81]

In all these respects, Yeats may be judged to have matured. In his early traffic with Rosicrucians and Cabalists, he is disarmingly easy to satirize as the adolescent enamored of ritual wardrobes, passwords, and the "pride of the adept"; the self-awareness of the later Yeats is, in the earlier, sometimes theatrical, posed. Yet the maturity is anticipated in certain persistencies—belief in the imagination, balance of sensibility and sense, moral courage. Like his contemporary, Irving Babbitt, Yeats could stand removed from the current intellectual orthodoxy without losing either his sharp sense of dissent or his own faith. He was not afraid to seem adolescent until he could achieve maturity on something like his own terms and win, by steadfast adherence, some respect for his outmoded causes. After 1900 we hear little more of arcane societies; Yeats turns from planning an occult ecclesiasticism to the organization of an Irish Theatre. The occult pursuits consolidate into a general defense of a more variously comprehensive universe than a positivist science will admit.

A central property of Yeats's religion which remains unchanged from youth to age is its lack of a consequent ethics. His old companion in theosophy, A.E., was fond of quoting the injunction, "For every step that you take in the pursuit of the hidden knowledge, take three steps in the perfecting of your own character." But Yeats, so far as one can see, never postulated an ascetical discipline preliminary to a religious experience. He had his moral code, and he had his ritual; but, as in primitive religions, the two were unrelated. Catholic Christianity is mystical, sacramental, ethical, and seeks, at whatever tension, to realize this character. With liberal Protestantism, the numinous disappears as *Aberglaube,* and religion becomes morality. In Yeats, religion returns to its pre-Christian and indeed pre-monotheistic character, becoming the search for knowledge of the unseen and for gnostic power.

Temperamentally, Yeats seems to have been an optimistic monist. If his magic seems generally 'white,' if he had no appetite for diabolism or blasphemy, he was correspondingly free from any sense of sin or need of redemption. In the broad sense, he remained, in *A Vision,* theosophic, by implication entertaining the belief in karma, reincarnation, and the eventual delivery from rebirth into the peace of nirvana; but it does not appear that his 'heart' ever accepted the Orient's pessimistic view of existence or the ethical release of the Four Noble Truths. Such a statement, however, needs modification; if the earlier Yeats identifies vision with reverie and virtue with abstention from Philistine ambitions, the later Yeats, with his doctrine of the will and its achievement of its True Mask, holds a more strenuous conception. And the later Yeats finds in the grasp of a "Vision of Evil" a chief differentiation between great poets like Villon, Dante (and himself), and such, for his last judgment, superficial poets as Emerson, Whitman, and A.E. Though his is a vision not of man's sin but of necessary pain, an unflinching view of world history which moves characteristically not by smooth progressions but by revolutions, reversals, and brutalities, it is an advance in Yeats's apprehension that he insists upon this realism.

1941

VI

NATHANIEL HAWTHORNE

I

CRITICS have sometimes talked as though a man could choose whether or not he will write with the grandeur of generality, whether he will choose native themes or cosmopolitan, whether he will write about himself for himself or of our common humanity and for all sorts and conditions of men. The question is academic, for no writer of rank can make such a choice. His vocation requires an eye single for the reception of what he sees. He cannot, by doctrinal resolves at the moment of composition, add a cubit to his stature. No author can make himself the complete man save by looking widely at the world of his own experience and deeply into himself and his intimates. The greatest novelists—Tolstoi, Dostoevski, Proust, George Eliot (in *The Mill on the Floss*)— have both width and depth; Hawthorne has, like Emily Brontë, a narrow canvas, but his pictures are ancestral and prophetic. He was a New Englander, and never, least of all in *The Marble Faun,* saw more than the New England conscience can discover; but he was never a local colorist, intent upon exploiting the 'quaint' in Yankee speech or mores.

During the twelve years after he left college, Hawthorne read copiously and widely, in French, English, and American literature and devoted attention concurrently to New England history. He acquainted himself thoroughly with the lore of Salem, especially of the witchcraft era; and it is to be regretted that he never wrote the history of witchcraft urged upon him, in 1845, by Evert Duyckinck. His concern with the Puritan past led him to Increase Mather's *Remarkable Providences* and Cotton Mather's *Wonders of the Invisible World* and *Magnalia Christi*. From the Athenaeum library, of which he became a 'proprietor,' he drew the local histories of Salem, Andover, Haverhill, Plymouth, Lynn, Scituate, Portland, and Nantucket and also volumes from the *Collections* of the Massachusetts Historical Society.

This study of New England history had deep instigation. Hawthorne felt the continuity of the present with the past, the sense that his own life and attitudes were inexplicable without a knowledge of the ancestral mind. The power apparent in his re-creations of the past lies in his imaginative identification with that past. By 1845 he had discarded as inadequate and external the historical romances of Scott, once his favorite author: "the world nowadays, requires a more earnest purpose, a deeper moral, a closer and homelier truth than he was qualified to supply it with." *The Scarlet Letter* is the historical novel more deeply conceived as an evocation of the spirit and the philosophy, rather than the speech and the costumes, of the past.

The "old, dull pain that runs through all Hawthorne's writing" disturbed Longfellow, his college classmate, and prohibited Emerson from reading his books. Against these reiterated charges, Hawthorne's family protested that the man was neither melancholy nor morbid. But clarifying is his son Julian's remark that Hawthorne the man and Hawthorne the writer, were as different as mountain from cloud.

[85]

Upon first reading the romances after his father's death, the son could not comprehend how the man whom he had known could have written such books.

This testimony, that Hawthorne's creative mind belonged to a different world from that of his private person, is corroborated by the testimony of his friends—Parker, Whipple, Alcott, and Loring; and Hawthorne himself was conscious of the dichotomy. His taste as a reader, so he wrote the publisher Fields, sought the opposite kind of novel from that which he himself could compose; and he singled out, as precisely suiting his appetite, Trollope's novels. He desired to write realistically and cheerfully. In the Introduction to *The Scarlet Letter,* he expresses surprise and distress that the result of his stay in the Salem Custom House should not have been an interpretation of the world about him: "The page of life that was spread out before me seemed dull and commonplace only because I have not followed its deeper import. A better book than I shall ever write was there." His sketches and notebooks abound in realistic delineation of peddlers, itinerant showmen, the catttle dealers at Brighton, the wild Irish women of Maine, beggars and other mendicants, the life of rural tavern and city hostelry; but these figures remain things seen and noted.

Hawthorne's marriage to Sophia Peabody appears to have proved completely satisfying; and one credits his avowal that she released him from the "dungeon" in which, for twelve years of self-captivity, he had languished.[1] But he did not

1. Hawthorne wrote Longfellow of the twelve years after their common years at Bowdoin: "By some witchcraft or other . . . . I have been carried apart from the main current of life, and find it impossible to get back again. . . . . I have made a captive of myself, and put me in a *dungeon,* and now I cannot find the key to let myself out." In *The House of the Seven Gables* he speaks of the "dungeon" of Hepzibah's heart.

marry until he was thirty-eight. Most of the ideas embodied in this fiction after 1842, the year of his marriage, can be found in the tales and notebooks written prior to that date—which is to say that Hawthorne's creative mind remained, in substantials, dominated by the same themes and the same attitude from the early *Seven Tales of My Native Land* to the uncompleted romances of *Septimius Felton* and *Dr. Grimshawe's Secret.*

What kept Hawthorne so long in his "lonely chamber"? He could never, subsequently, explain it save under the metaphor of witchcraft or enchantment. At Bowdoin, he had been mildly convivial and addicted to shooting, fishing, and cards; the intimate of Horatio Bridge and Franklin Pierce, whose campaign biography he later, and to the scandal of New England, composed. But, returned to Salem, he found his widowed mother withdrawn into ceremonial seclusion, his sisters following her example; and passivity to circumstance led him into the same conventual routine. Doubtless, pride was his principal jailor. The romancer hated the city of his lonely youth, characterizing it as "chill east wind and the chillest of social atmospheres." The Hawthornes, once eminent in town and colony, as their descendant believed, were now poor and forgotten, eclipsed by the merchant princes of the East India and China trade, who, in the first decades of the nineteenth century, had erected their three-story brick and white-porched mansions on Chestnut Street. Feeling himself the equal of these magnates, yet sensitive to possible slights and affronts, he would not encounter them and became, contrary to his family's allegiance and that of other reputable citizens, a Jacksonian Democrat.

Pride and isolation acting upon articulate sensibility begot an art compounded of introspection and observation; the *Twice-told Tales* are, half, probings into the human heart—specifically Hawthorne's; half, mildly shrewd or mildly sentimental delineations of scenes and persons seen by a young man during his solitary walk at sundown.

Of this remoteness from his kind, Hawthorne was at least partially conscious. In some of his most powerful tales he projects his sense of proud isolation—notably in the characters of Wakefield, Ethan Brand, and Chillingworth. The 'unpardonable sin,' the sin against the Holy Ghost, which, because the Bible does not define it, became for many introspective New Englanders an ominous shadow, was, for Hawthorne, the sin of analyzing human hearts without loving them, that "cold tendency" attributed to Coverdale, which made him "pry with a speculative interest into people's passions and impulses." Even at the end of Hawthorne's life the theme obsessed him; and in Septimius Felton he again created out of his former self, the isolated introspectionist. According to the English poet Allingham, who knew Hawthorne in his consular fifties, Hawthorne never wholly overcame his early remoteness. "Sometimes I don't love him so well; his attitude of *spectator ad extra* strikes a chill." If Ethan Brand was not self-portraiture, he was undoubtedly the man Hawthorne might have become.

His interest in the theme of inheritance, the past as it lives on to blight the present, had, too, its origin in Hawthorne's experience. The Fall of the House of Pyncheon was the Hawthornes' fall. Like the Pyncheons they had their lineage and their curse. Major William Hawthorne, the "grave, bearded, sable-cloaked and steeple-crowned proprietor," who landed with his Bible and his sword in 1630, was a bitter

[88]

persecutor of the Quakers, for whose deeds his descendant sought to make reparation in "The Gentle Boy." His son, Judge John Hawthorne, played a relentless role in the martyrdom of the witches, one of whom invoked upon the Judge and his children's children that curse which "the dreary and unprosperous condition of the [Hawthorne] race, for many a long year back, would argue to exist." The Eastern Land Claim, occupying central importance in the plot of the *Seven Gables,* translates the Hawthornes' never realized right to nine thousand acres in Maine, deeded to their ancestor, in 1666, by an Indian sagamore.

A curse, 'great expectations,' the persecution of Quakers and witches: such was Hawthorne's inheritance. Did he really believe that some doom hung over him? Questions concerning Hawthorne's literal beliefs are not to be bluntly resolved. A novelist has the latitude of imaginatively projecting states of mind, giving experimental fulfilments to what in the man are but hints and implications. Doubtless all a novelist's characters which possess appreciable reality are portraits from sketches of himself.

The philosopher must decide between alternatives or reduce his thesis and antithesis to some underlying or overlying synthesis. But the novelist of a speculative turn need not push his positions to a stand. He can divide his conflicting insights between his characters, as Hawthorne does in the discussion of the Fall of Man which develops the implications of Donatello's conversion. The comments he offers in his own name do not wander far from orthodoxy; but he allows Miriam and, later, Kenyon to expound the conception, assuredly entertainable, that sin, like sorrow, may be "merely an element of human education, through which we struggle to a higher and purer state than we could otherwise have attained."

In Hawthorne's own mind there lingered elements of the irrational, unknowns, and inexplicables which remained to the end obscure. Without faith in Christian creeds or communions, his mind held fast to the older apprehensions of the universe. He took no stock in those 'celestial railroads,' Unitarianism or Transcendentalism, nor yet in the monomania of the abolitionists. Half skeptic and half fideist, he believed the insights of Calvinism to be deeper than the moralism of the Boston Brahmins or the visions of the Concord seers. In Hawthorne as in no other American writer, Puritanism, freed from its doctrinal precisions, took central position. Though his secular self could scarcely avow them, in his novels and tales his beliefs, those of his haunted mind, could bespeak themselves unashamed.

The problem of sin was of absorbing interest. Whatever the implications of *The Scarlet Letter* may be, the moral for its author did not lie in Hester's words upon which the modern reader seizes, her words to Dimmesdale that "what we did had a consecration of its own." In the Conclusion to the novel, he says: "Earlier in life, Hester had vainly imagined that she herself might be the destined prophetess of sounder relations between the sexes, but had long since recognized the impossibility that any mission of divine and mysterious truth should be confided to a woman stained with sin, bowed down with shame, or even burdened with a life-long sorrow." Hawthorne does not describe the adultery but only the consequences for the two persons—upon the one, open shame; upon the other, of concealed.

Like the Catholic church, Hawthorne regarded the sins

of the flesh as less heinous than those of the spirit: his real villains are Judge Pyncheon, Ethan Brand, and Chillingworth. But he was chiefly engaged with the primal and general corruption of the human heart—what traditional Christianity calls 'original sin.' Moreover, he passed from act to motive and intention. In the spirit of the Sermon on the Mount, he believed that "whosoever looketh upon a woman to lust after her hath already committed adultery with her in his heart." A man does not cease to be a sinner because, through circumstances or cowardice, he does not act upon his impulses.

II

The method of the tales and romances is an allegorical symbolism: concept or person epitomized in some physical object. The scarlet letter, the brilliant flower of Zenobia, the false teeth of Westervelt, the ears of Donatello, Hilda's doves, the minister's black veil, the 'bosom serpent' of "Egotism." The relation between symbol and thing symbolized is frequently the relation of the physical to the spiritual. In Hawthorne's notebooks, the hint which was developed into the tale of "Lady Eleanore's Mantle" reads: "To symbolize moral or spiritual disease by disease of the body:—thus, when a person committed anything, it might cause a sore to appear on the body." Later, in analyzing the malady of Dimmesdale, he speculated: "A physical disease which we consider as something separate and apart may be after all but a symptom of disorder in the spiritual part of our nature."[2]

To one acquainted with the writings of Swedenborg,

2. The sentence from "The Leech and His Patient," chap. x of *The Scarlet Letter*, is effectively quoted by Dr. Smith Ely Jeliffe, *Sketches in Psychosomatic Medicine* (1939).

widely known among the American and English Transcendentalists, this obsession of Hawthorne's will suggest the doctrine of 'Correspondences,' according to which all the objects of the physical world owe their existence to the states of thought and feeling of which they are the perpetual symbols. The doctrine is poetically expounded in a chapter of Emerson's *Nature;* a similar doctrine was preached by Charles Fourier, the French socialist whose views won final sovereignty at Brook Farm. But the founts and origins of Hawthorne's symbolism are Spenser and Bunyan. At six, the boy used to read *Pilgrim's Progress* by the hour. The early impression was ineffaceable: *Pilgrim's Progress* is the one book to which the unallusive Hawthorne constantly alludes in his own writing; and in conversation its 'Slough of Despond,' 'Doubting Castle,' and the like seem to have served himself and his family as their private communal language. Without doubt, it was Bunyan who begot and nurtured that moral allegory which became Hawthorne's mode of vision in his most characteristic tales. For the *Faerie Queene,* the first book purchased with his own money, he cherished, too, a lifelong affection.

Wanting to deal with the deep and the subtle in civilized man, Hawthorne sought to find, in literary tradition, usable, expressive structures. Inner states must, for artistic purposes, be given objectification. The general equation suggests itself that a haunted house is like a haunted mind; the mind has its labyrinthine ways, its secret recesses; the terror of the body pursued through space is a mirror of mental terror as one is pursued by an obsession.

The technique available to Hawthorne as a narrative writer concerning the states of the soul was, primarily, the technique of the Gothic romance. Hawthorne read the novels of Godwin, *Caleb Williams* and *St. Leon,* and the romances of Mrs. Radcliffe, Maturin, and Brockden Brown as well as Scott; and the remark of Hawthorne's sister that, during his years of Salem solitude, he read a great many novels and made an artistic study of them, must surely be taken to include the Gothic novels. "Virtually all the methods and devices peculiar to the Gothic romances reappear in Hawthorne's romances and most of the Gothic character types also....."[3] Hawthorne's villains are descended from the villains of Mrs. Radcliffe, Godwin, and Brockden Brown.

Hawthorne has himself indicated his lineage within prose fiction by calling his work 'romance' and by expressly distinguishing this from the realistic novel: "When a writer calls his work a Romance, it need hardly be observed that he wishes to claim a certain latitude both as to its fashion and material." The romancer may use "The Marvellous"—that is, the supernatural, and it is his characteristic also to "connect a bygone time with the very present." Hawthorne alludes to the distinction between 'romance' and 'novel' as one already familiar, not of his own devising. In her *Progress of Romance* (1785), Clara Reeve thus distinguished the species: "The Novel is a picture of real life and manners, and of the time in which it is written. The Romance in lofty and elevated language describes what never happened nor is likely to happen." In the early decades of the nineteenth century there appeared a series of reprints called the "Romanticists'

3. Cf. Arlin Turner, "Hawthorne's Literary Borrowings," *PMLA*, LI (1936), 543 ff.; and especially N. F. Doubleday's perceptive study of "Hawthorne's Use of Three Gothic Patterns," *College English*, VII (1946), 250 ff. Miss Birkhead includes Hawthorne as well as Poe in her *Tale of Terror: A Study of the Gothic Romance* (1921).

and Novelists' Library"; and Montague Summers, in his *Gothic Quest,* prints an amusing recipe for translating the Gothic 'romance' into the realistic and bourgeois 'novel.'

There are two special requirements for the romance. The first is the sense of the past. This is present in all Hawthorne's novels except the *Blithedale*. The *House* and the *Faun* are, to be sure, set in the present; but by varying means they lead one back into the past. The Pyncheon house is presented to us as an ancient mansion inhabited by a family of ancient lineage, a slowly decaying line of aristocrats; and the frequent throwbacks to the generations of the family in the seventeenth- and eighteenth-century generations are intended to give this historical dimension. Set in the period of the American Revolution, *Septimius Felton* moves back, in the story of the Great Sachem and that of Sir Forrester, to the American Indian and the end of the Middle Ages.

The second requirement is mystery—or the sense of the supernatural. Among the Gothic romancers, there were two schools of thought: one, led by Mrs. Radcliffe, held that the mysteries should all be cleared up at the end; the other, headed by Monk Lewis, permitted the unrationalized supernatural. At the end of *The Marble Faun*—or rather, at the beginning of chapter l, its original ending—Hawthorne remarks: "The gentle reader, we trust, would not thank us for one of those minute elucidations, which are so tedious, and often, after all, so unsatisfactory in clearing up the romantic mysteries of a story"; he is certainly thinking of such explanations as Mrs. Radcliffe offers in the final chapters of *The Mysteries of Udolpho* and *The Italian*—explanations which the reader assuredly finds inadequate to the shudder produced when one saw a statue drop blood or heard shrieks from a room closed for centuries or music from a ruined crypt.

Hawthorne does not wish to explain all at the end. He has two chief ways of giving a sense of the mysterious while offering a concurrent rationale. One is to offer alternative natural and supernatural explanations—as, for instance, with the incision of the letter *A* upon the breast of Dimmesdale—generally attaching the latter to the credulous speculations of the community, the fanciful gossip of the uneducated, yet meanwhile intimating that the gossip may be wiser than the science. The other is to suggest that the 'supernatural' may be subsumable under natural law. Like Barrett Wendell after him, Hawthorne inclined to believe that witchcraft and allied manifestations of magic were not imposture or delusion but such phenomena as were subsequently studied by societies for psychical research or medical science. The mysterious death of the Pyncheons is by apoplexy; the mysterious power of the Maules is seen to be what the 1830's and 40's knew as mesmerism or hypnotism. "Modern psychology, it may be, will endeavor to reduce these alleged necromancies within a system instead of rejecting them as altogether fabulous," writes Hawthorne of the theory that in the dream world the Maules ruled the Pyncheons.

Nearest to the Gothic novel are Hawthorne's posthumous romances, *The Ancestral Footstep, Septimius Felton,* in the theme familiar from Godwin's *St. Leon, or the Elixir of Life,* and especially *Dr. Grimshawe's Secret;* and there is something indeed strange and inviting to speculation about this return—something pathetic about this occupation, during the Civil War and at the end of life, with these somewhat mechanical and external mysteries.

In *Dr. Grimshawe's Secret,* Hawthorne indeed specifies that Braithwaite Hall "had not much of the stateliness of one of Mrs. Radcliffe's castles, with their suites of rooms opening one into another"; but in spite of this disjoinder he has succeeded in making the place adequately sinister and labyrinthine. We shudder when, upon the disappearance of the guileless American claimant, the leader of the rescue party hails Lord Braithwaite with the melodramatic words: "Not thus do you escape your penalty, hardened and crafty one! I demand .... access to the secret ways of this mansion, of which thou dost unjustly retain possession. I shall disclose what for centuries has remained hidden,—the ghostly secrets that this house hides." And we discover that there is indeed a trap door operated by a mechanism in the wall and beyond that a door with a mysterious spring, admitting into a secret chamber containing a macabre and ghostly figure which crumbles into dust as we look and a golden coffer to be opened by a long-sought key.

The book's villain, Braithwaite, has the advantages of being not only an Italian but a Catholic, employing for his own sinister purposes the service of a priest-chaplain. In his 1824 essay on Mrs. Radcliffe's works, Sir Walter Scott attributes to her and her novel *The Italian* the innovation of Catholic mystery: "She selected the new and powerful machinery afforded her by the Popish religion, when established in its paramount superiority, and thereby had at her disposal monks, spies, dungeons, the mute obedience of the bigot, the dark and dominating spirit of the crafty priest,—all the thunders of the Vatican and all the terrors of the Inquisition." One remembers that Hilda's disappearance is explained by her imprisonment in a convent because of an old ecclesiastic's "mistaken hope of a proselyte." Meanwhile the deeply memorable passages in the novel explore the experience of the American claimant, the passionate pilgrim to England, at once revolted by and drawn to the ancestral race—explore, too, the states of illness and sleep.

It may be affirmed that *Grimshawe's Secret,* Hawthorne's "English romance," would have been a combination of realistic psychology—an analysis of the feelings of an American in England—and a Gothic plot.

III

If we turn back to *The House of the Seven Gables* we have an instance of Hawthorne at almost his best—at what he indeed thought to be work more characteristic of him than *The Scarlet Letter.* This is a book which gains from re-readings, though the defects more clearly differentiate themselves as well.

Hawthorne's strength lies in his central myth—the situation of a declining aristocratic family contrasted with youthful vigor and adaptation—and in its psychological realism; its weakness is in its plot and in its narrative method.

His method is almost that of a succession of tableaux. The characters do not really develop or change; and we do not find it easy to remember their speech, for Hawthorne has no considered notion of what parts of his story to put into dialogue, what not. Nor does he show us the characters acting on each other, as James does in *The Golden Bowl.* Here, as elsewhere, Hawthorne arranges scenes of conversation, ordinarily between two persons, but they are expository, do not advance the action. James says of Hepzibah that "she is a picture as her companions are pictures." A few of the characters have their symbolic attitudes—the Scowl and the Sultry Smile; there is a sense of the blondness of Phoebe and the somber brunetteness of Hepzibah. Hepzibah, dimly related to Hester, Zenobia, Miriam, and Sibyl Darcy, is a tragedy queen in faded silhouette.

The point of view is clumsily managed, for the novel professes to be narrated by an "I" who presently passes into a "we," a narrator whose relation to the characters in the story and whose sources of information are never elucidated—indeed, an "I" or "we" so shadowy as ordinarily to be forgotten and certainly irrelevant. The mind of no character is consistently used, though Hepzibah and Holgrave are probably the predominant reflectors; Hawthorne makes no attempt to tell his outer story of three centuries through the consciousness of Hepzibah and Clifford. Yet he never really gains by his liberties of omniscient commentator. His own moral reflections on the fable, for example, are substantially uttered in the speeches of Holgrave and, for the last chapters, of Clifford; or, more accurately, they are divided between all the principal characters excepting Hepzibah, a consciousness felt by Hawthorne too dim to afford any general illumination. It is, in point of fact, Hepzibah who suffers most from the narrator's underlining and expostulations. Without his showman's pointing and nudgings, Hawthorne has 'realized' her character; and in chapter ii he is as superfluous as tasteless and heavily humorous: "Far from us be the indecorum of assisting, even in imagination at a maiden lady's toilet..... The maiden lady's devotions are concluded. Will she now issue forth over the threshold of our story: Not yet, by many minutes." This chapter is a kind of preparation for the yet more melodramatic technique of the chapter, "Governor

Pyncheon," in which the Judge is rhetorically interrogated as, dead from apoplexy, he sits in his chair.

The 'plot' of the novel has to do with the warfare between the ancient families of Pyncheon and Maule, the dying curse of Maule that God may give the Pyncheons blood to drink, the mesmeric power of Maules over Pyncheons, illustrated by Matthew's power over Alice and Holgrave's over Phoebe, the mysterious land claim and the mysterious portrait, and the plot of Judge Pyncheon against his cousin Clifford. But Hawthorne is not really much interested in this initial mechanism. As *The Scarlet Letter* starts after the guilty act is over and is concerned with the effects of sin, not with its perpetration, so all this plot is but to set in action something else which is Hawthorne's real plot—the effect of pride, poverty, and suffering upon two old aristocrats.

The 'plot' is viewed as an unavoidable nuisance. It is certainly managed with great awkwardness. In *The Marble Faun* two endings were still unequal to the rescue of the plot from its surrounding and overpowering art commentary, character analysis, and philosophical discussion. In the leisurely *Blithedale Romance,* the melodramatic plot—which concerns the villain Westervelt and Old Moodie (*alias* Fauntleroy) and the identity of his daughters, Zenobia and Priscilla—is crowded into a pair of hasty chapters late in the book, as difficult to recall as Hawthorne found embarrassing to manage.

The *House* properly begins with chapter ii, "The Little Shop Window." But Hawthorne fumbles through a first chapter somewhat after the fashion of a Scott opening; he hurriedly sketches Pyncheon history and mystery, inserting an episode from the eighteenth-century history of the family as a tale allegedly composed by Holgrave. James has offered the suggestive comment that the *House* seems less a great novel than the prologue to a great novel; perhaps he should have said epilogue. One can imagine Hawthorne's scenario as expanded to the dimensions of such a family saga as *Buddenbrooks*. But what we actually have is an expanded novelette covering some three months, which could take still further retrenchment and which represents the past only by implication and dramatic utterance.

Though the *House* is partly 'romance,' partly 'novel,' its strength lies in its delicate realism. With impunity and by aid of a critically subtracting memory, we can extract its Gothic plot: we can remove the theatric controversy with the Maules; disengage the inserted tale of Alice Pyncheon, the proud lady with the prouder father, who are humiliated by their contemporary Maules; forget the portrait and the mysterious and death-portending music of Alice's harpsichord, and the mesmeric phenomena. The story then reduces itself to something like this: A New England aristocrat is so reduced in means that, having already been forced to take in a talented but radical young lodger, she must now resort to the more blatant expedient of shopkeeping. On the same day a wholesome and cheerful young relative arrives; on the following day there returns, after thirty years in prison, the old lady's sensitive brother. A rich and harsh relative calls one day to intimidate the brother into showing him the location of a missing document; thwarted in his wish, he dies of apoplexy. In their terror at the sight, the old brother and sister run away, though happily they return—concurrently with the young lodger and the young relative—before the body is discovered by the world.

The central characters are Hepzibah and Clifford, both admirably keyed though treated with somewhat repetitious exposition. And the relationship between the two is perceptively defined: the reversal of roles which makes the woman the less aesthetic of the two; the adjustment of the woman to the distaste her grotesqueness occasions her brother. Both are types of aristocratic decline, too ineffectual in a hurrying world to make insistent their claims to aristocratic status. Clifford's aestheticism is passive, appreciative, and even perhaps limited largely to foods and wines and flowers and fragrances. Hepzibah lacks all aristocratic equipage except pride; in ability she is inferior to her inferiors, cannot even manage. The Fall of the House of Pyncheon is not a tragic but a pathetic fall: the house is about to end, not with a bang but with a whimper. Actually it ends, less dramatically, with a 'happy ending' which does not seem false—since it is really happy only for the young people, who, renew, with plebeian blood, the decayed stock; while for the elderly celibates there is no real hope. To the central characters, Phoebe and Holgrave offer foil and contrast; and the hens in the garden tender their mildly comic parody.

The most effective chapters in the book are those which concern Clifford, a characterization singled out for praise by Pater, a successful Clifford, in his essay on Coleridge, a Clifford of genius: the chapters called "The Guest," "The Arched Window," and "The Flight of the Owls." Though Hawthorne approaches Clifford more lightly than he does Hepzibah and the Judge, one could yet spare his commentary. His romance would gain much in artistic precision and purity —and, through purity, power—if it were pruned severely of Hawthorne's underlinings and pointings.

The book is damaged by the presence—or the handling—of Judge Pyncheon. Hawthorne's villains, from Butler in *Fanshawe* on, are the really manufactured characters. As Randall Stewart has remarked, they are "nearly all persecutors of women or of men of feminine weakness." They are lovers of cruelty to whom the weak are both repellent and at the same time fascinating objects. If we ask why these sadists are not made convincing, we must say that Hawthorne presents them in a mode alien to his general mode of characterization. He either ought to render them exclusively from the point of view of their victims—Dimmesdale's view of Chillingworth, Clifford's of the Judge—or ought to give, from within, the sadist's views. In the *House,* everyone is successively seen from inside, seen with some sympathy, except Pyncheon. He is given, that is, an exterior with no interior; he thus seems out of scale, out of key, with the other characters.

Hawthorne's Gothicism was customarily as unfortunate as his allegory despite his endeavors to subtilize and interiorize the Gothic machinery and the Gothic characters. The finest passages in Hawthorne's novels are passages of psychological insight into ethical or emotional states or into characters of generally autobiographical cast like Dimmesdale and Clifford and Coverdale and Redcliffe. An admirable and little known example is the analysis in *Grimshawe's Secret* of Edward's mental states during his illness and his subsequent slow recovery.

Hawthorne's true line of development is shown by such subsequent writing as that, various enough, of Pater (especially in his *Marius* and *Portraits*) and James and Proust—writers of the psychological novel concerned with the mysteries of the human soul. Hawthorne was possessed, surely, by a belief that our mysteries are more important than our knowledges. Once, in *The Scarlet Letter,* he trusted to find adequate mystery in "The Interior of a Heart." He never again felt that confidence in the power of character to unfold its own plots.

1941

VII

FRANZ KAFKA

KAFKA'S novels evoke a world as self-coherent and characteristic as that of Dickens, of Dostoevski, of Proust, of Poe, of Hawthorne. Like Hawthorne's and Poe's, Kafka's is a limited, a lyric, world. Kafka is a metaphysical poet in symbolist narrative.

His is a city world. Like Dickens' London, it flourishes in grotesques. But they have not the vigor, the delight in their own salt being, of Quilp and Miss Mowcher; and they are chiefly unnamed and seen but momentarily. Old women look out of inquisitive windows; in the gutters sit leering irreverent mocking children; a young lad, his nose half eaten away, scrutinizes arrivals; the warden wears a gross body, ill-adjusted to his "dry bony face, with a great nose twisted to one side."

It is an overcrowded, airless world, within which it is difficult to sustain faith in the weight and worth of the individual. In Georg Salter's illustration to *The Trial,* most persons except the introspective hero are but shapes of shadow. Kafka's solipsism is intelligible, is defensible, as necessary to sustaining, in a city of the anonymous, the belief that the soul and its choices matter.

Even Kafka's imagined America is not a land of broad cornfields shining in the sun but a chiefly metropolitan affair, already stratified, weary, and hopeless—a land of hotels and of slums. "Karl thought of the east end of New York which his uncle had promised to show him where it was said that several families lived in one little room and the house of a whole family consisted of one corner where many children clustered around their parents." Kafka read Franklin's *Autobiography,* we are told, and admired Walt Whitman, and liked the Americans because he believed them to be "healthy and optimistic." But his imagination does not so present them. A sort of W.P.A. theater opens hospitably at the end, to be sure; yet the novel follows Dickens, not Alger. Karl is the young Copperfield, the young Oliver Twist, the sensitive boy ejected from home on charges which puzzle him. He finds America gleaming but hard. Before landing, he encounters social injustice in the case of "The Stoker"; his uncle, who suddenly appears and assumes his support, as suddenly and less plausibly renounces responsibility; he is deceived and maltreated by his chance traveling companions: for no fault of his own, he is discharged from the hotel; he comes near to ending as a slavey in a delirious apartment. America is a world in which elevators whiz up and down, phonographs play incessantly without anyone's listening, political candidates get lost in the crowds which are to elect them. It offers the image of the ascent to Brunelda's apartment: long stairs moving up into squalid darkness; beside the stair-railing, a little girl weeps, then rushes up the steps gasping for breath.

Kafka's is a world known in nightmares—a rational, unnatural world in which unnatural situations are rationally worked out—in which everyone is able, like Lewis Carroll's creatures, to argue long, ingeniously, and convincingly. It is a nightmare world in which the "I," all innocent and eager to submit, all desirous to propitiate, is pushed about, pursued, regimented by potencies veiled of visage—in which one is forever being orally examined by dignitaries who forever flunk one. The self and the world are juxtaposed in opposition. If one is not being pursued by the world or carried off by the world, one is running after it. There is the image of the old father trying to catch the ear of the Castle dignitaries—trying in vain, for the officials go at a gallop, their carriages "race like mad." It is the world of a Mack Sennett comedy—one of chase and pursuit, of intense movement, horizontal and vertical: of running and climbing. It is a world of uncertainty and insecurity, of fear and trembling.

It is a world of hierarchy, created by Kafka in the parodic imitation of the Austrian bureaucracies under which he lived, within which, as underofficial, he worked. In its chief traits it could be a feudal estate or it could be an American department store or a chain of restaurants or a metropolitan public library. Hierarchy provides, negatively, for deferment of responsibility or infinite regress. One's complaint always reaches the wrong office; one is passed on from office to office, in general moving up the scale of delegated authority, only to find that the proper official to handle the complaint is out of town, or the necessary documents are lost, or by delay one's claim is outlawed. Wonderful is the efficiency of an order so complexly gradated that every expert is inexpert at satisfying the simple need for justice.

There are other difficulties. Hierarchic order is necessary in a universe densely populated, whether with atoms or souls; yet, in an order so intricate, instrumentalities must, almost unavoidably, turn into ends: readers exist in order that librarians may make card catalogues, pupils in order that educationalists may publish books on Methods of Teaching, worshipers in order that janitors may sweep and lock churches. Underofficials, those who administer the rules to the public, can scarcely be expected to understand the spirit of the rules or what, as formulated by unseen and doubtless long dead 'higher-ups,' the rules aimed at. A teeming universe must, of course, be a 'planned,' even if an ill planned, or a too fussily planned, society. The easy improvization which fits the New England village cannot be transported to the city. Indeed, by one of his most brilliant audacities, Kafka imagines that even the Village cannot really be a village, for if its multiple needs are adequately to be taken care of, there will be business enough to require busy attention from a whole caste of officials.

Kafka's novels can be taken as burlesques of bureaucracy. Satiric of course they are. Yet they lack satiric norm, a contrasting model of elegance and humanity. The hero is too uncertain of himself to sit in judgment on duly constituted authorities and too intent upon learning their ways to have leisure for criticizing them. As for bureaucracy, it is even at its worst a corruption of order; and order is a state so blessed, so indispensable, that even its parodies deserve respect. As for bureaucrats, the common charge against them is that they are too insistent upon the importance of their work, too narrow in their conception of it; but surely it is the duty of officials to be officious, and narrowness and even scrupulosity are marks of their being dedicated to their profession. The work of the world is carried on by experts, not by gentlemen; and if we want to deepen the sense of "work" and "world," we must add, "strait is the gate and narrow the way"; the price of salvation is the forced sale of all that one has.

Hierarchy is pyramidal. Is there, for Kafka, any Reason, any Supreme Will, at the top and the end? Or is hierarchy a staircase which ends not in a dome or a tower but in a fall into darkness? The answer is uncertain. Of a chief justice we never hear or of a head-manager of a hotel. In *The Castle,* we hear for a preliminary moment of the "Count West-west," but soon he and any direct view of the Castle itself are lost or forgotten. Doubtless there is an ultimate authority, but we never reach it except through its intermediaries: there is no direct vision. In "Before the Law," the lowest doorkeeper can see a few doors ahead of him into what he believes to be a vast series of ascents: "From hall to hall keepers stand at every door, one more powerful than the other. Even the third of these has an aspect that even I cannot bear to look at." Of the ascending series we can say that there is no point at which we observe it to stop. Olga explains to K.: "Who is it that Barnabas speaks to there [in the Castle] I have no idea—perhaps the clerk is lowest in the whole staff; but even if he is lowest he can put one in touch with the next man above him, and if he can't even do that he can refer to somebody who can give the name." They are men set under authority; and "Does not the least degree of authority contain the whole?"

In both *The Trial* and *The Castle,* underofficials, advocates, and villagers spend much time in speculating upon the ways of the 'higher-ups.' In the latter we hear Amalia ask, "Is it Castle gossip you're at? .... There are people in the village who live on it; they stick their heads together just like you two and entertain each other by the hour"; to which K. replies that he is just such a person, "and moreover people who don't care for such gossip and leave it all to others don't interest me particularly." So the talk goes on. We "gossip" or

[108]

speculate about Klamm, attempting to adjust to coherence the glimpses we catch. A man like Klamm "who is so much sought after and rarely seen is apt to take different shapes in people's imaginations"—to give rise to theophanies very diverse each from the other.

Yet Kafka's officials, however otherwise various, have in common a certain obtrusive perversity, their lack of elegance. So, too, the rooms in which the courts sit have none of the grandeur or even decent neatness we might anticipate, and the Castle is unimpressive, disappointing to strangers. Instead of being better balanced and more humanistic than the villagers, the officials are officious, pompous, and pedantic. But the "virtues of the pagans are splendid vices": "officious, pompous, and pedantic" are dyslogistic terms to be transvaluated as "conscientious, dignified, and properly accurate."

These paper-reading officials are scholars, intellectuals; and their scholarly life bears no discernible relation to their biological and affective lives: they have their mistresses; and they have their papers.

"Papers," we see, both bless and curse. They are not only the records of law and the ledgers of business but the annals of history and the memory of the race, the possibility of preserving and interpreting our past experience. They represent the effort of the intellect to understand by dissection, arrangement, systemization. "Papers" constitute civilization; without them we remain barbarians. Yet they clutter up the world and menace our freedom. They may be "busy work" to amuse old children, to keep scholars from thinking and the timid from knowing themselves afraid. The academic vice is the substitution of 'research' for existential thinking; to preserve records without selection, to multiply discriminations until one is incapable of singleness of mind and simplicity of action. Papers assemble, by the most laudable of intentions, into libraries; yet for every man who, like Arnold, fears he may know more than he feels, a great library must be an object of terror—a monument to the futility of past speculation, a deterrent to future action.

There are some rich, fantastic scenes in which Kafka's papers become objects in themselves, figures in a Disney cartoon: in *The Castle* the search through the superintendent's bedroom for a missing document—in the process of which papers half cover the floor and go on mounting—or the description of Sordini's office, every wall of which is covered with columns of documents tied together, piled on top of one another; "those are only the documents that Sordini is working on at the time, and as bundles of papers are continually being taken away and brought in, and all in great haste, those columns are always falling on the floor, and it's just those perpetual crashes, following fast on one another, that have come to distinguish Sordini's workroom."

The copiousness of the papers has an approximate correspondence in the volubility of official speech. Ready argument characterizes almost all Kafka's people—not merely his lawyers and secretaries. In these novels all are dialecticians: all are conscious of *pro et contra,* fertile in 'various lections.' Unlike Mann's controversialists, Naphtha and Settembrini, who argue in abstract terms, Kafka's are existential thinkers and deploy their subtlety on the obscure and difficult matter of how to live aright.

The Trial and *The Castle* are composed very largely of dialogues, and dialogues dialectic. Indeed, the characteristic excitement of these later novels, written by a student of Plato and Kierkegaard, lies in the wit and intellectual suspense of the dialogue. No more than the papers in Sordini's office do the thoughts stand still; like the action in a murder mystery, they move by sudden shifts of direction, convincing evasions of the foregone conclusion.

What does Kafka intend us to make of his argumentation? Is it ridiculously specious, or—so far as it goes—true: "Both" would have to be the answer. It is absurd to speculate about the nature of the highest, for of course we cannot know; we cannot even know how near we come to knowing. Yet it is man's true nature and highest function to engage himself upon these speculative questions concerning the nature of reality; and there can be no delegation of this duty to others.

Kafka's world is one of mystery. In stories like "The Country Doctor" and "Metamorphosis," the unnatural thrusts itself into the orderly sequence of nature. The redaction of a young clerk into a bug neither allows of allegorical sterilization, nor is presented as a dream. It is the chief horror of the story, perhaps, that no one within it sees what happens as "impossible"; it is horrible, to be sure, but in various ways these people, obviously sane and simple, adjust themselves to a painful situation. There are occasional bits of near or even sheer magic in Kafka: in *The Castle,* Barnabas disappears with the rapidity of an elf or a thought; the first day passes and it grows night, within an hour or two after morning; after a few days of living with K., Frieda, formerly "unnaturally seductive," is withering in his arms. But it is not Kafka's ordinary or best practice thus to deal in legerdemain. He secures his sense of mystery chiefly through his device of multiple interpretation.

His method offers a superficial analogy with that of

Hawthorne. But Hawthorne offers alternatives—usually supernaturalism and some form of naturalism. Thus, at the elaborate ending of *The Scarlet Letter,* we are tendered the preliminary option of supposing that there was, or was not, a scarlet letter imprinted upon the breast of the minister, and then a choice of three methods for the possible production of the stigmata: by the natural means of penance; by means of magic and drugs; or by the outgoing operation of the spirit. "The reader," says Hawthorne, "may choose among these theories."

It is not Kafka's method thus to contrast a supernatural with a natural reading. It is, for him, in and through the natural that the supernatural operates and, with whatever intermittence and illusion, is revealed.

Kafka's world is neither the world of the average sensual man nor yet fantasy. It is the world seen slightly askew, as one looks through his legs or stands on his head, or sees it in a distorting mirror. Nor does his adjustment take, like Swift's in *Gulliver,* the method of segregation. With Swift, the fantastic is safely corralled and tucked away in the initial assumption; with Kafka, realism and fantasy move in more close and sensitive relation. In *The Trial* and *The Castle* the whole sequence is so improbable as to suggest some kind of pervasive allegory, but at no point (or almost no point) does one encounter downright impossibility. It is improbable that any law courts of a wealthy city should be lodged high up in dingy tenement houses or that a village should require the service of a vast staff of busy, hurrying officials, or that, upon looking into a lumber-room in one's own office building, one should discover two court-wardens being flogged. Yet these things "could be"; they are not like centaurs, oceans flowing with lemonade, and trees growing greenbacks. And Kafka's multiple interpretations are all possible options within one world. They represent the same fact or situation read from successive views, as the operations of a mind which keeps correcting itself.

Kafka offers a convincing interpretation; then, with rapidity, substitutes another, yet more convincing. A scene in *Amerika* shows Robinson, his face and arms swathed in manifold bandages. "It was horrible to see him lift his arms to his eyes to wipe away his tears with the bandages—tears of pain or grief or perhaps even of joy at seeing Karl again." Then we see the horror dissolve. "The trivial nature of his wounds could be seen from the old rags of bandages with which the lift-boys, obviously in jest, had swathed him round."

The Castle abounds in more subtle shifts. A woman sits in a chair in a kitchen. The pale light gives a "gleam of silk" to her dress; she seems to be an aristocrat, "although of course illness and weariness give even peasants a look of refinement." To a question from K., the woman replies disdainfully, but "whether contemptuous of K. or of her own answer was not clear." If one is self-conscious or otherwise fearful, it is necessary and difficult to interpret the looks of others. Thus K. sees the peasants gazing fixedly at him; he thinks it done out of malice—yet perhaps they really wanted something from him but could not express it, or, perhaps, on the other hand, they were simply childish. But if the first view of the peasants and their attitude was mistaken, what about the first view of Barnabas? One doubt, one disillusionment, infects the judge with a general mistrust of his judgment. "Perhaps K. was as mistaken in Barnabas' goodness as in the malice of the peasants." Frieda's hands "were certainly small and delicate, but they could quite as well have been called weak and characterless." After Olga's account of Amalia's defiance of Sordini, K. says, "Amalia's act was remarkable enough, but the more you say about it the less clearly can it be decided whether it was noble or petty, clever or foolish, heroic or cowardly." Longer, more structural examples are the discussion between K. and the Superintendent concerning the meaning of Klamm's letter, and K.'s talk with Frieda about the landlady, and Olga's discussion with K. regarding the nature of Barnabas' relation to the Castle.

Kafka's 'mystery' is, then, the apparent sign of how elusive is the truth. What happens is tolerably easy to ascertain, but what it means is precarious as well as important.

Such scrupulosity of interpretation recalls a characteristic feature of hierarchy everywhere prominent in Kafka's novels —the connection between promotion, pleasing, and propitiation. Kafka's worlds are patriarchies or theocracies. One's success or failure depends on one's skill in divining the wishes of the great man; and among underlings there develops a necessary skill in calculating his mood by his complexion, step, tone of voice. Cases there naturally are in which the signs allow of differing interpretation between experts.

The interpretative complexity recalls also the elaborations of rabbinic and patristic commentary. John Mason Neale's commentary on the Song of Songs offers, out of innumerable Fathers, Doctors, and Saints, all manner of conflicting yet severally edifying glosses: on the text, "his left hand is under my head, and his right hand doth embrace me," for example. What is the distinction between the hands, and why their positions? According to some, the hands distinguish temporal from spiritual goods; according to another view, the left hand equates the law, the right hand the gospel; according to another, the left hand indicates punishment, the right, blessings and rewards. Other comments differentiate mystical states—the left being the Illuminative as the right is the Unitive Way. And "the loveliest interpretation of all," says Neale, is that which sees in the left the Manhood of Christ, and in the right his Godhead.

Not until late in his life did Kafka begin to study the *Talmud;* but already, in the priest's discourse at the Cathedral (*The Trial*), Kafka shows his ingenuity and depth as the exegete of a given fable. The priest cites the studies of innumerable rabbis who had already concerned themselves with the story. "I am only showing you different opinions about it," he says. "You mustn't have too much regard for opinions. The text is unchangeable and opinions are often only an expression of doubt about it." Like Kierkegaard, whose *Fear and Trembling* starts from and repeatedly returns to the story of Abraham and Isaac, so Kafka, delighting in speculation, yet offers his story as a mythic fable the meaning of which is anterior to and unexhausted by any included commentary.

Myth is not allegory; and Kafka is not an allegorist. An allegory is a series of concepts provided with a narrative or a narrative accompanied by a conceptual parallel. Strictly, it is a philosophical sequence which systematically works itself out in images. But allegory is rarely as pure as *Pilgrim's Progress* or *The Romance of the Rose:* it deviates from purity in two directions—by losing its systematic character, becoming a series of intermittent symbolisms; or by keeping its system but abstaining from offering a conceptual key to its parable.

[115]

The novels of Kafka are not, in any exact sense, allegorical. From his diaries and aphorisms and his friend Brod's commentaries, we know that he intended the novels to give creative expression to the mysteries of Justice and Grace; that they are 'metaphysical' novels we should surely have discerned without aid. But Kafka provided them with no conceptual chart; they require none; and it is their special richness that they have much particularity untranslatable into generality. We need not systematically recall that the Castle is Heaven or that K.'s disappointments show the mysterious ways in which God moves. The ways of men are, for men who seek to understand them, baffling enough.

Kafka's symbols are, indeed, capable of more than the religious interpretation. According to Brod, K. symbolizes the Jew, in his exclusion from society and his eagerness for inclusion, as well as the seeker after the Kingdom of Heaven. But K. is also the bachelor in search of marriage and companionship; and K. is also every man in respect to his final aloneness.

The novels all, significantly, remained unfinished. Of them Kafka wrote: "What sense would there be in reviving such .... bungled pieces of work? Only if one hoped to create a whole out of such fragments, some complete work to which one could make a final appeal....." We have for each novel, however, a notion of the ending. *Amerika* was to conclude with the young hero's finding, within the Nature Theatre of Oklahoma, his freedom, "even his old house and his parents." *The Trial* is of Brod's assembling, and a chapter like "The Whipper" could only vaguely be placed. Parts of the novels—for example, "The Stoker" and "Before the Law"— were published separately.

With some plausibility, one might call these books novels of the spiritual picaresque. Yet they are not completely episodic: even in the loosest, *Amerika,* the two rascals, Delamarcke and Robinson, reappear after we suppose ourselves to have seen the last of them; and in *The Castle* there is a very considerable integration of the materials: one notes in particular the fashion in which the matter of chapter i (the teacher, the Lasemann family, Hans Brunswick and his mother) is subsequently developed. Each novel begins in substantially the same way: the hero breaks with his past. In two of them he has left his home, and we meet him as he enters a new world; in a third his thirtieth birthday and his summons collaborate to start a new life.

The question of method is: Can there be a logic of composition when one's theme is the irruption of the irrational? There might, of course, be a psychological unwinding; the episodes might grow more complex, deeper, or more wry. In the unfinished state of the novels, no such progress is obvious. If one compares these novels with the mystical documents of SS. Teresa and John of the Cross, he finds no such obvious symmetry and development as that of *The Interior Mansions.* Such systematic structure was too rational for Kafka.

It is Kafka's narrative method (with occasional lapses) to write from within the mind of the hero. The introspective hero, through whose eyes we have glimpses of other persons, static figures, is man alone, man hunted and haunted, man confronted with powers which elude him and with women with whom he is never at ease, man prosecuted and persecuted. He is the man eager to do right but perpetually baffled and thwarted and confused as to what it is to do right—the man for whom the sense of duty, of responsibility, the irreducibility of 'ought,' has survived the positive and particular codes of religions and moral systems—the man in search of salvation.

A narrow, moving writer, Kafka is both an artist and a symbol. The appeal of this symbol has been extraordinarily wide to Europeans and Americans in the past decade. One secular hope after another has failed. Kafka can be the symbol for what is left. He is illiberal, unrelenting, unsentimental; as Spender has said, he combines the power of the visionary with the self-criticism of the skeptic, so that he communicates the sense of there being something to believe without the claim of being able to define what it is. It is difficult today to believe in the reality of a world of comfort, good sense, and progress; we doubt that we shall ever see such a world again; we think it wise to prepare ourselves spiritually for worlds more exacting and metaphysical; and of such worlds Kafka is initiate.

1941

VIII

E. M. FORSTER

THE English novel has traditionally admitted of no exact definition, no generic purity. Written by all sorts and conditions of men, as was the poetic drama of the Elizabethans, it has been designed for as many kinds of readers. The responsibility of the nineteenth-century novelist was to offer his readers a 'story'; apart from that, and within the bounds of Victorian taste, he might provide what *extras* he would—sociological, psychological, moral. Sweeping his puppets aside, he might preach the new ethics, expound the nature of things, prophesy the future actions of his characters or the future of human character; returning again to his puppets, he was free to pass in and out of their minds, now seeing through this pair of subsidiary eyes, now through that, now exerting the omniscience of his own sight.

At the end of the century the popular novelists continued the practice; but George Moore and Henry James, both aliens to England, both trained in France, felt dissatisfaction at such looseness. A genre so readily susceptible of illustrated homily on prison reform or the loss of clerical faith lacked minimal aesthetic dignity. They busied themselves—James in particular—in devising an 'art of fiction.' Of this gospel the chief dogma was that of the 'point of view.' The novelist, James held, must preliminarily decide through whose eyes the proposed narration may, most profitably, be viewed. Or he may, instead, decide to use a series of instruments in turn: the ten books of *The Awkward Age* utilize the vision of as many persons. But there must be no mere convenient, unpremeditated transit. Further, the author must rigorously exclude himself as public commentator or 'chorus.' The only point of view inadmissible is that of the author.

James's technical experiments have, properly, commanded the respect of subsequent artists; and his influence upon them has been impressive. Consciousness of form has marked the work of authors otherwise so various as Gide, Joyce, Hemingway, Mrs. Woolf. *Les Faux-Monnayeurs* is a novel analyzing the composition of a novel; each section of *Ulysses* employs a different method and a different style; Hemingway has removed from the novel all save its public or behavioristic device, its dialogue. Mrs. Woolf has subtracted almost all the banks which define the stream of consciousness; she has practiced the limited vision, successive instruments of vision; in *The Waves* she has offered in place of dialogue a series, symphonically arranged, of interior soliloquies. Like Proust's, like Huxley's *Point Counterpoint,* her work seems to aim at musical form—a pattern of recurrent and recurrently enriched motifs.

E. M. Forster has full and appreciative acquaintance with the work of Gide, Proust, Joyce, and Mrs. Woolf; but his personal masters are, rather, Jane Austen, Samuel Butler, and Dostoevski. In his *Aspects of the Novel* (1927) he expounds the Jamesian theory only to reject, or to minimize, it. It is dangerous, he thinks, for the writer to take the reader into his confidence about his characters; but "to take your reader into your confidence about the universe is a different thing.

It is not dangerous for a novelist to draw back from his characters, as Hardy and Conrad do, and to generalize about the conditions under which he thinks life is carried on." To be sure, the novelist must not anticipate, publicly, that future end of his characters which he must, out of elementary artistic decency, foresee. As the characters develop, the author interprets, concomitantly, their states of sensibility; he must keep his dramatic or factual surprises until they reach, and take on or off their guard, his persons. But it can impair no proper aesthetic faith that the novelist should articulate such observations and insights upon humanity at large as the conduct of his personae may suggest. Indeed, if the novelist be a man of wisdom as well as mimetic power, his imaginative self can assuredly, only with loss, be spared from the dramatis personae. He should move among his characters, though certainly not as man among dolls; he is to be cast as the most deeply seeing member of a company.

Both in theory and in practice Forster declines to restrict the novelist's ancient liberties. The richness of the novel, for him, lies in its range of levels. There is the 'story'; then there are the persons of the story who act and speak; then there is the 'inner life' of the characters, to be overheard and translated by the author; and, finally, there is the philosophic commentary of the author.

Plot, characters, philosophy: each has a life of its own and threatens to expand until it menaces its competitors. If the novel restrict itself to action and speech, it does no more than reduplicate—and with the subtraction of mimes present 'in person'—the drama or even the biography. To avoid being less, the novel must be more. "A memoir," says Forster, "is history, it is based on evidence. . . . . And it is the function of the novelist to reveal the hidden life at its source: to tell us more than could be known. In daily life we never understand each other; neither complete clairvoyance nor complete confessional exists. . . . . But people in a novel can be understood completely by the reader, if the novelist wishes; their inner vision as well as their outer life can be exposed."

If, on the other hand, the 'inner life' become all, then, like some parts of Proust's *A la Recherche,* the novel turns into a psychological treatise and the persons decompose into their constituent moods and 'intermittences.' The too intense self-consciousness, the self-consciousness divorced from action, dissolving its object, discovers no residual self.

In *Howard's End* the Wilcoxes are characterized as people incomplete because they eliminate the personal, cannot say 'I'; but Helen Schlegel, overconcerned with the subconscious self, speaking of mankind as puppets whom an invisible show-man twitches into love and war, herself risks, though by an opposite method, the elimination of the personal.

To Forster, then, the novel has its own function, that of a persuasive equilibrism: it must balance the claims of the existence and the essence, of personalities and ideas. To Forster, values are more important than facts; and the real values are friendship, intellectual exploration, insight and imagination, the values of the 'inner life.' But observation and interpretation, though terminal values, are, biologically, parasitic upon the body and the life of action. Forster's own work very satisfyingly preserves this equilibrium both in its repertory of characters and in its narrative method.

Even more than the drama, the novel suits the mind which pushes beyond gossip and news but is unable or unwilling to accept a creed. Such a mind habitually generalizes its insights but, through indolence, self-distrust, or skepticism of absolutes, attempts no thoroughgoing system. It goes beyond judgments of John and John's attitude toward Jane to the conception of types—men like John and men who have such attitudes toward women like Jane; its propositions are not universals about men and women but linger halfway between John and 'all men.' Forster's essays, assembled in *Abinger Harvest* (1936),[1] document the conclusion that he has ideas but no 'idea.'

In *Howard's End* he expresses the view that the complexity of the modern world offers to the best-prepared and best-intentioned but an option of alternative visions: seeing life steadily *or* seeing it whole. His own choice is clearly the latter; like Santayana, he has the excellent manners, the freedom from exaggerated emphases and extravagant exclusions, which traditionally have been the marks of the humanist.

Santayana's *Last Puritan* showed unexpected lapses in comprehension. Though it saw value in man as animal (Lord Jim), as epicure (Peter Alden), as social creature (Mario), as high-minded spectator (Oliver), his catholicity failed to see any 'life of reason' in New England Brahminism. Forster's range of 'partial sympathies' is even greater. Though his cardinal virtues are courage, candor, sympathy, insight, disinterestedness, he can find worth in almost every quality

1. Like the *Dickinson,* the book of essays is disappointing to a Forsterian. Its eighty constituent parts should, if their author deemed them all worth reprinting, have been collected in five or six thinnish volumes addressed rather to pockets than library shelves. The two sketches of Howard Sturgis and Ronald Firbank are deft and discerning; "My Wood," a parable on the effects of owning property, is a little masterpiece; "Liberty in England," Forster's address before the International Congress of Writers at Paris, has a finely simple candor and dignity. But too many of the pieces, though stylistically meticulous, produce the impression of a coy sprightliness alien to the novels. Without a mask, pushed to the front of the stage to make his speech, Forster grows self-conscious.

except humbug and muddledom. People are "far more different than is pretended," says wise Margaret Schlegel, who loves her Philistine husband, to her sister Helen, an unmarried mother. "All over the world men and women are worrying because they cannot develop as they are supposed to develop. Here and there they have the matter out, and it comforts them..... Develop what you have; love your child. I do not love children. I am thankful to have none..... And others—others go further still and move outside humanity altogether..... It is part of the battle against sameness. Differences—external differences, planted by God in a single family, so that there may always be color; sorrow perhaps, but color in the daily grey." Only, different as human beings are, they have the common obligation of self-knowledge. Those who "follow neither the heart nor the brain, and march to their destiny by catch-words" are the truly benighted. "The armies are full of pleasant and pious folk. But they have yielded to the only enemy that matters—the enemy within. They have sinned against passion and truth, and vain will be their strife after virtue."

Forster's England is chiefly that of the upper middle classes and the intelligentsia of the universities and London, an England exempt alike from Lady Catherine de Bourgh and from the sadistic peasants of T. F. Powys, a world set on 'gold islands.' From this world, cruelty and lust are almost absent. The vice of the bourgeois, as Arnold and Carlyle never wearied of pointing out, is self-complacent, unimaginative respectability; the vice of the intelligentsia is another form of Phariseeism: the snobbery of 'culture.'

Poor culture! We recall, as one of its exemplars, Miss Austen's Mary Bennett, who, "being the only plain one in the family, worked hard for knowledge and accomplishments, [and] was always impatient for display." In Forster's novels, 'culture' appears as the Rev. Cuthbert Eager at Santa Croce, lecturing to English lady tourists with "prayer books as well as guide-books in their hands"; as Cecil Vyse, who acknowledges the truth of Lucy's impassioned analysis: "You may understand beautiful things, but you don't know how to see them; and you wrap yourself up in art and books and music, and would try to wrap me up"; as poor lower-class Leonard Bast, who read Mr. Ruskin, spouted R.L.S., tinkled a little Grieg, and "hoped to come to Culture suddenly, much as the Revivalist hopes to come to Jesus."

One of Forster's short fantasies concerns the 'Celestial Omnibus,' driven now by Sir Thomas Browne, now by Jane Austen, now by Dante, and conducting the candidly imaginative to the land of vicarious experience, where Achilles and Mrs. Gamp and Hamlet and Tom Jones disport themselves companionably. A 'boy' makes the journey in innocence, because he is too ignorant and wise to attribute the experience to his personal 'merit.' Not so Mr. Bons, Surbiton councilman who owns seven copies of Shelley. Rich in his spiritual possessions and conscious of how they set him above his fellows, Mr. Bons invokes the great Dante: "I have honored you. I have quoted you. I have bound you in vellum." But in vain; for poetry is means and not end. Poetry is a spirit, not to be won like a degree but to be cherished like a flame. And those who, like Mr. Bons, do not *connect* their conduct with their 'culture,' will, like Mr. Bons, topple from the precipice of heaven into a junk-heap of glittering fragments.

Elementary 'culture,' the pathos of isolated aspirants, lists, with an epithet or two apiece, the books it has read. "Give me a list of books, worth-while ones," it bids the professor; "I want to improve myself." "How whimsical Lamb is." "Henry James, how subtle." "Should I read Thackeray next, or Tolstoi?" Culture is a list of books.

Then there is that more rarefied culture which keeps up with the newest ideas and the latest names, which is allusive and light of touch, which, in order to play dexterously about the peripheral, takes the central for granted—the 'clever' culture of people who live for books, concerts, art shows, and chatter about them. "In spite of the season, Mrs. Vyse managed to scrape together a dinner-party consisting entirely of the grandchildren of famous people. The food was poor, but the talk had a witty weariness. . . . . One was tired of everything, it seemed. One launched into enthusiasm only to collapse gracefully, and pick oneself up amid sympathetic laughter."

The 'real thing' of which 'culture' is the parody or the pastiche appears in Forster's novels also. It is represented by Cecil and Tibby, more completely by Philip, Ricky Elliott, and Mr. Beebe. These men are all ascetics, scholars, aesthetes; are all, in varying degrees, detached observers, contemplatives. They are not, Forster makes clear, capable of passion for women or indeed, perhaps, for persons at all. Tibby is a scholar for whom the human is tiresome and crude, who desires the passionless air of knowledge. Ansell is a professional philosopher, who believes it "worth while to grow old and dusty seeking for truth though truth is unattainable, restating questions that have been stated at the beginning of the world."

Cecil, the comic hero of *A Room with a View,* is a born

curator. Wrong in seeking to pervert the nature of others, wrong in being so ignorant of his own nature as to 'make love,' in himself he is a genuine, if restricted and indoor, person. The Middle Ages would have understood Cecil and have made a place for him. "He was mediaeval .... well educated, well endowed, and not deficient physically, he remained in the grip of a certain devil whom the modern world knows as self-consciousness, and whom the mediaeval, with dimmer vision, worshipped as asceticism. A Gothic statue implies celibacy, just as a Greek statue implies fruition." Cecil does not fit 'Nature': he is a muff at sports; he is to be imagined, thinks Lucy, as in a drawing-room, one with drawn draperies. His one attempt at love-making turns into high, rueful comedy. "As he approached her, he found time to wish that he could recoil. As he touched her, his gold pince-nez became dislodged and was flattened between them." Cecil's pince-nez was genuine; his passion, secondhand and temporary.

Yet, ludicrous as this scene displays him, Cecil is absurd only as he pretends to a range of feelings denied him. Forster's books house few 'flat' characters, to be summarized in a gesture or a recurrent phrase; for as we are just about to catalogue them, they turn toward us another side, a side which surprises us but surprises us in a way which is compatible with the sides' being sides of the same person. When Lucy eventually rebels against Cecil's attempt to mold a Vyse out of a Honeychurch, she treats him to a ruthless portrait of himself. He is unexpectedly, convincingly, honest and grateful. He cannot change his character; but, for the first time, he recognizes it.

Where Angels Fear to Tread offers Philip, a contemplative

of larger stature. The short book is yet long enough to show Philip's growth from a culture-snob, vain of his taste for art and Italy, vain of his emancipation from British provincialism, into a man of insight and good will. Philip becomes capable of imaginative sympathy with persons as alien as the son of an Italian dentist; he grows in humanity. But his final triumph is self-awareness; and to this recognition he, like Cecil, is helped by a woman whom, in his ignorance, he fancies he desires. He sees all, 'appreciates' all, but cannot act. To Caroline Abbott he confesses: "You would be surprised to know what my great events are. Going to the theatre yesterday, talking to you now—I don't suppose I shall ever meet anything greater. I seem fated to pass through the world without colliding with it or moving it—and I'm sure I can't tell you whether the fate's good or evil. I don't die—I don't fall in love .... you are quite right; life to me is just a spectacle."

This is perhaps the best which 'culture,' singlehanded can achieve. To know "the best that has been said and thought in the world"; to know with any fulness, to make one's own, the thought and experience of Aristotle, Lucretius, Racine, Montaigne, Bossuet, Goethe, Sophocles, Plotinus, Confucius, Aristophanes, Dante: that would be a formidable 'task.' The outlines of the knower's personality would grow vague; he would have no appetite left for life, no capacity for action, no energy for creation; he would be infected with a sense of personal futility. "Tout est dit: et l'on vient trop tard depuis plus de sept mille ans qu'il y a des hommes, et qui pensent."

There are times when, by reaction, Forster turns, temporarily, to primitivism—as Philip turns to Gino, as Rickey turns to that child of nature, his half-brother, Stephen. An animal is better than a prig, that parody of the saint; a child is better than a prude. But then Forster sees, too, the virtues of downright, unashamed, healthy extroverts like Henry Wilcox and Son, men devoid of intellectual curiosity and extra-domestic sympathy who can 'do' and build. Himself a habituate of the 'inner life,' Forster feels, as must all half-men aware of their incompleteness, the attraction of his opposites: the child, the animal, the Philistine. Himself English, he has felt the fascination not only of Italy but of Italians—warm, spontaneous Italians, untroubled by scrupulosity or the miasma of introspection, affectionate by impulse not duty.

But Forster's humanity will know all: the earth, passion and friendship, thirst for the truth, and hunger for the Absolute. For him, the 'Greek view of life' is the right one; and the problem of morality is not to set mind against body or soul against either, not to antithesize but to reconcile, by proportion and subordination to effect a harmony. In the language of metaphysics, Forster must be described as a 'naturalist'; but, he is a 'naturalist' with wings and humanistic manners and balancing perceptions, one who, like Santayana, believes that everything ideal has a natural basis and that nothing in nature is incapable of an ideal fulfilment.

Is this balance attainable by the individual? That is to ask whether the individual can exemplify the universal man; and the answer seems clear: never completely; often not at all. Yet it is the undeniable nisus of large natures. Forster's character who most closely approaches universality is Margaret Schlegel: though she possesses her own personal mark and stamp, she can comprehend natures as diverse from her own as Mrs. Wilcox, Helen, and Henry; and she achieves the triumph not only of marrying a Philistine but of achieving with him a marriage of spiritual union. Then there is Forster's friend and hero, Lowes Dickinson, who admired the versatility of Goethe, who himself longed to be a poet, a scientist, and a dominating figure in European politics, yet who, doomed to dondom, expanded his vision through his friendships with men of affairs and philosophers and painters. "He solved his particular problem in later life by developing the power of entering into other people's positions while he retained his own....."

Forster's 'humanist,' Mr. Jackson, warns Ricky that the Greeks were not broad church clergymen, that Sophocles was not a kind of enlightened bishop. If there is a 'golden mean,' it is not what so often passes for it—tepidity or compromise or apathetic good humor. "The business man who assumes that this life is everything, and the mystic who asserts that it is nothing, fail, on this side and on that, to hit the truth. 'Yes, I see, dear; it's about halfway between,' [the Schlegels'] Aunt Juley had hazarded in earlier years. No; truth, being alive, was not halfway between anything. It was only to be found by continuous excursions into either realm, and though proportion is the final secret, to espouse it at the outset is to insure sterility."

Much which passes for 'the mean' is not virtue, one must agree. There is no virtue in low vitality, intellectual or moral indolence, unwillingness to think one's thought to its end, cowardice in failing to take one's stand. To be moderate is not glibly to utter, "It takes all sorts to make a world" and forthwith to give up definition and distinction. Moderation is an achievement, not an endowment. Its pursuit necessitates the exercise of the will, checking this excessive impulse and that disorderly propensity; and the really central man must have a passion for proportion.

The doctrine of the mean needs a modern re-examination. G. K. Chesterton used to argue that equilibrium was the character of a sound society, like that of the Middle Ages, when the monk was bidden to be as pacific as possible and the knight to be as warlike as he could; and such a conception finds support in Plato's *Republic*. Shall we say, rather, that every man must seek to be the 'balanced' man? This was undoubtedly the doctrine of the *honnête homme;* but, outside the confines of a leisure class, it is almost impossible to apply.

One might, of course, chart out his day so that all the chief values received representation; one might do his 'daily dozen' at calisthenics and dialectics and social intercourse and prayer. Gamaliel Bradford's meticulous regimen gave a half-hour to French, another to Greek, another to the piano, and so on through a half-prescribed horarium. But this seems somewhat mechanical as well as meticulous; and it seems doubtful whether such precision is advisable outside of a monastic community. A week of solitude and hard thinking or writing, followed by a week of society (with a capital letter or a small) might be a kind of balance more appropriate to the life of a man in the 'world.' "The great rule," says von Hügel, "is, Variety up to the verge of dissipation: Recollection up to the verge of emptiness: each alternating with the other and making a rich, fruitful tension."

Is proportion to be thought of in terms of the day, the year, or the lifetime? Forster votes for the last of these conceptions; and, by his passage from mysticism to politics and back again, his youthful thrusts into many directions, his subsequent mellow maturity, Lowes Dickinson, who said, "I shall be at my best in old age," best illustrates Forster's thesis that "proportion is the final secret."

Common to Dickinson and Forster is the belief that reason is neither the foundation of knowledge (which is animal faith) nor its spire (which is intuition). "It is difficult for most of us to realize both the importance and unimportance of reason. But it is a difficulty which the profounder humanists have managed to solve." Complete rationalism, like glaring sunlight, dries up the vegetation. Complete credulity produces so lush, so rank a growth of vegetation that the human way is lost, the human stature dwarfed. The lamplit table is surrounded by darkness, an unknown to be neither apostasized nor denied. What science and intellect can tell us can be said; the rest, which, too, must be articulated, can be uttered only in myth and poetry. Dickinson and Forster are equilibrists and mediators. As the human or the historical context seems to require, they affirm the achieved known or the limits of 'exact knowledge' and final function of the imagination.

Forster's earlier novels, *Where Angels Fear To Tread* (1905), *The Longest Journey* (1907), and *A Room with a View* (1908), of which the first and the third are high comedy, keep to the sunlight of realism. With *Howard's End* (1910), however, Forster introduces what his friend Dickinson called the 'double vision,' the sense of this world and a world or worlds behind. *A Passage to India* (1924) came between two volumes of fantasies, *The Celestial Omnibus* (1923) and *The Eternal Moment* (1928). In all these works there is an element which might loosely be called mystical, the brooding presence of worlds unreachable by the ordinary processes of the mind. Yet these 'intimations' are not to be thought of as breakings-in of a supernatural 'Other,' and no theology is adumbrated. Sometimes the tales suggest abnormal psychology, psychic powers rarely possessed; sometimes they are fanciful, symbolical expositions of the nature of things. In several of them, a myth of the 'future life' envisions the real values attainable now.

In none of his tales does Forster attempt to suggest a diabolic supernatural; and, in all save the frankly parabolic sketches of the 'future life,' he restricts himself to what, in action, belongs to the normal. He has written no *Lady into Fox,* that fantasy at the end of which no reverse metamorphosis occurs. Nor has he used Hawthorne's sometimes routine supplying of alternatives, natural and magical: Donatello had, or had not, the ears of a faun; there was, or was not, an actual scarlet letter visibly incised on Dimmesdale's breast or visible as portent in the heavens. The element of fantasy, with Forster, is conveyed not through a mechanism but through a coloring: ordinary existence is illuminated by the white light of eternity or the blue light of 'value,' so that the familiar landscape gains an arresting strangeness.

Two tales, "The Eternal Moment" and "The Road from Colonus," contrast existence and reality: all that matters in life may happen in a day or an hour; and even the experiencer may afterwards forget this normative moment. Sometimes the tale presents, in heightened contrast, the opposition between sense and sensibility, between the Philistine, even of the kind which teaches Virgil or quotes Dante, and the impractical romantic, who may not have read the poets but who can see into the life of things. Mr. Worters, the Englishman of great possessions, of 'public school' culture and conventional churchmanship, owns a copse of beeches which he equips with fences and neat paths and a bridge, all the accouterments for destroying its small wildness, so cherished by his fiancée and an inefficient young man. Disillusioned by 'culture,' the girl runs off into the woods. "On the Other Side of the Hedge" from the world of unanalyzed efficiency and uncritical belief in 'progress,' she discovers the world of happy leisure. "Where does this place lead to?" "Nowhere, thank the Lord." Though frequently they contain a flight, it would be crass to bear down on these tales as so many escapes. Escape is a form of criticism in these tales; and the goal of the flight and its starting-point offer an opposition and a contrast in values. In essence, the tales are all parables addressed to the Philistine who, like Mr. Wilcox, fails to "connect" prose and poetry, who has never seen that art and religion cannot be assigned to museums and churches but must be apprehended through participation in the same spirit which prompted the painter and the saint.

In both *Howard's End* and *A Passage to India* the central figure is that of an old woman without cleverness or articulateness who appears but briefly yet whose presence attends and pervades the book. Mrs. Wilcox and Mrs. Moore are studies of the same type. Both have, intermittently, telepathic and clairvoyant power. Recognizing in Margaret Schlegel a spiritual heir to her own feelings for her country home, Mrs. Wilcox bequeaths it on an unsigned scrap of paper; the sensible Wilcoxes, knowing the testament to possess no legal validity and thinking the act was of momentary aberration, pay no heed to it. But, without design, Margaret becomes the second Mrs. Wilcox, comes (in spite of obstacles) to live at Howard's End, and, on the last page of the novel, learns by chance, from her husband, that the house had been left her.

Says Margaret to her sister: "I feel that you and I and Henry are only fragments of that woman's mind. She knows everything. She is everything. She is the house, and the tree that leans over it. People have their own deaths as well as their own lives, and even if there is nothing beyond death, we shall differ in our nothingness. I cannot believe that knowledge such as hers will perish with knowledge such as mine. She knew about realities."

Mrs. Moore visits India, where her son is a British official. Shortly after her arrival, she goes into a mosque to feel God's presence, falls into conversation with a young Moslem physician, journeys to the Marabar Hills on an excursion which he arranges. While within the caves, she is made ill by the echoes, and her son's fiancée has the hallucination of having been assaulted by the Moslem host. Mrs. Moore refuses to testify at the momentous trial of the Indian, and leaves the country, dying on the journey; but she has massively impressed the perceptive, whether Western or Eastern, who knew her. No presence is so real at the trial as hers; her name becomes Indianized into Esmiss Esmoor and reverberates, like that of a Hindu goddess, through the crowd; votive tombs spring up; she is accepted as one Westerner who comprehended the East, who was indeed an Oriental; the goodness of Mrs. Moore, which had amounted to nothing more tangible than her good will, survived, in the heart of the Moslem Aziz, his bitter abandonment of further traffic with the English. Like Mrs. Wilcox, Mrs. Moore 'knew.'

How did these women know, and what did they know? The answers are left vague. Mrs. Wilcox loved the soil and the garden and her house; she was a goddess of place, a local spirit in whom, apparently, the personal was transcended.

There is (Forster seems to say) the level of consciousness and selfhood, to which some human beings never ascend; and there is a level above the personal which looks down upon it with loving impersonality. Without any practical knowledge of how to unite, politically, the many contending, contentious sects of Indians, or how to reconcile the Indians and their imperial masters, Mrs. Moore affirms the oneness of all humanity.

In both women there are elements of what Forster, in his *Aspects of the Novel,* calls the 'prophetic.' The center of *A Passage,* structurally and psychologically, is the excursion to the Marabar Caves. The drama of the novel, the trial, springs from it; but what happened there affected, permanently, the lives of all the excursionists. Dickinson, as well as others, asked Forster: What really happened in the caves? The author does not say—not, I think, for the reasons which led Hawthorne to leave vague so much in *The Marble Faun,* but because he has made it sufficiently clear that no assault on Adela took place. What happened, to Adela and to Mrs. Moore, was the hysterical experience of the caves, bare, dark, echoing. The echo is that of eternity, infinity, the Absolute, which for optimistic Shaftesbury and Pope might seem to say:

> All Nature is but Art unknown to thee;
> All Chance, Direction, which thou canst not see;
> All Discord, Harmony not understood;
> All partial Evil, universal Good.....

To fatigued Mrs. Moore, on the contrary, it murmured: "Pathos, piety, courage—they exist, but are identical, and so is filth. Everything exists; nothing has value." "If one had spoken vileness in that place, or quoted lofty poetry, the comment would have been the same—*ou-boum*..... Religion appeared, poor little talkative Christianity, and she knew that all its divine words from 'Let there be Light' to 'It is finished' only amounted to 'boum.' " "She had come to that state where the horror of the universe and its smallness are both visible at the same time—the twilight of the double vision in which so many elderly people are involved. If this world is not to our taste, well, at all events there is Heaven, Hell, Annihilation. .... All heroic endeavor, and all that is known as art, assumes that there is such a background, just as all practical endeavor, when the world is to our taste, assumes that the world is all. But in the twilight of the double vision, a spiritual muddledom is set up for which no high-sounding words can be found; we can neither act nor refrain from action, we can neither ignore nor respect Infinity." "Visions are supposed to entail profundity but—Wait till you get one, dear reader! The abyss also may be petty, the serpent of eternity made of maggots. ....." The Absolute may be a demon.

The skeptical blight which descended, as infernal vision, upon Mrs. Moore is possible, doubtless, only to one reared in the Christian tradition. This skepticism insinuates that human values have no basis in the nature of things; that our moral distinctions are factitious; that the universe mocks sinner and saint alike; that both our aspirations and our intellections are folly in the presence of the blind if not malevolent destiny which begat us.

Mrs. Moore's first sentiment in India was to feel the unity of all religions; her second, to feel the futility of all. Upon all save the steadiest and soundest minds, the effect of sojourn *in partibus infidelium* must be a bland tolerance, or an insular bigotry, or the reduction of all morality to mores. The older generation of missionaries to India were, like the English civil officials, too little given to distinguishing between what was British and what was Christian, too contemptuously intolerant of alien faiths; the newest generation suffers from the opposite danger of making too few discriminations. The echoes from the caves of cosmopolitanism say, with sentimentality or with cynicism, that all moralities and all religions stand on the same footing of priest-craft, ruler-craft, traditions, and custom. The serpent of eternity whispers, Ye shall be like gods, knowing not good from evil.

In his life of Dickinson, Forster declares that his two visits to India were "wonderful" by reason of the happiness and peacefulness he found, and he disagrees with his friend's judgment that "There is no solution to the problem of governing India. Our presence is a curse both to them and to us. Our going will be worse." Yet, in his candor, the novelist has offered testimony to this painful conclusion. Even such English 'liberals' as Fielding and Adela and such a well-intentioned Indian as Aziz fail of mutual understanding. Between the masses of rulers and ruled, only hostility and suspicion exist. And, divided by their religions, Moslem, Hindu, Sikh, Jain, the Indians cannot achieve a national unity. On this note, the novel ends.

Leaving India, Fielding lands at Venice. He doubtless speaks for Forster when he contrasts romantic India with classical Europe, "the civilization that has escaped muddle." "The Mediterranean is the human norm. When men leave that exquisite lake, whether through the Bosphorus or the Pillars of Hercules, they approach the monstrous and extraordinary....."

Yet the novel offers a chastened hopefulness. Mrs. Moore

and her younger children, who share something of her nature, do 'reach' this alien world even if they do not intellectually comprehend it. Personal relationships are precious; and, though nation misconceives nation, individuals can pass the boundaries into intuitive communion.

In *The Passage,* as in his two high comedies, Forster shows an extraordinary capacity for disinterested observation which plays alike over Indians, Italians, and English. His "Notes on English Character," the inaugural essay in *Abinger Harvest* (1936), shows the same capacity. The English, he says, are essentially middle class and 'public school,' not unfeeling but afraid to feel, not unemotional but slow of emotional response, moral rather than religious, self-complacent, muddle-headed. The English character is not vicious and not really cold, but it is incomplete. But then, "No national character is complete. We have to look for some qualities in one part of the world and others in another." This perception gives Forster the basis for the amiable satire with which he treats the more ludicrous of international misunderstandings. The position from which the satire is urged is that of a complete and balanced human nature which has never been incarnated in race nor even in individual, but which the critic, like the novelist, can imaginatively conceive.

Without bigotry or bitterness, Forster has endeavored to attain wholeness and steadiness of vision; his passion is for dispassionate comprehension.

Neither at wholeness nor at steadiness do his novels completely succeed. There are wide and deep *lacunae:* except for the Basts, there are no poor. From poverty, hunger, lust, and hate, his people are exempt. Love between the sexes, though recognized with sympathy, is never explored and is central to none of his novels. Except in *A Passage to India,* the individual is not portrayed in relation to society: Church and State, institutions, communal causes which engage men and draw them out of themselves, do not engage and draw his self-aware individuals.

Forster's 'double vision' allows him that modulation from crisp comedy to a delicate pathos, the passage from prose to poetry and back again, which is his prime quality. But the gift has its perils; and he does not always succeed in keeping the two worlds in proper focus. *Howard's End,* in many respects his most mellow and mature performance, fails centrally, just here. The titular theme of *genius loci* is too vague, too 'mystical,' to bear the weight placed upon it, just as Mrs. Wilcox, who embodies it and is intended to pervade the novel, does not succeed in doing so. Sometimes Forster's forays into the land behind reason bring him only to the "misty mid-region of Weir," the realm of romantic fantasy. In *A Passage to India,* on the other hand, the 'double vision' gives depth and perspective. The two worlds need not, however, appear explicitly. In the earlier novels, prose and comedy hold the stage; the 'poetry' is in the imaginative lighting of the action. Forster's adjustments are various and varyingly successful; but his constant consciousness of levels, levels of experience and of knowledge, gives the vibration of life to his work.

His production has been sparse—five novels in a lifetime; it is unlikely that there will be others. Except for *A Passage to India,* the ostensible theme of which attracted attention, his work has had no wide popularity; yet he is not a proper object for the peculiar devotion of a cult. Witty, sensitive, epigrammatic and metaphorical, he never becomes precious. He rather conceals than obtrudes his defects and mild perversities; conscious eccentricities he is without. Though he lacks power, the deficiency is felt only upon retrospect; for his subleties, instead of springing apart as separate perceptions, reticulate into substance. Aided as he is by the preservative of style, it is probable that his fine distinction will survive some more strident originalities of our day.

1937

IX

HENRY JAMES

SYMBOLIC IMAGERY IN THE LATER NOVELS

THE general occasions of the 'last period' are tolerably clear, if scarcely of the same order of being. There is, first, the gradual loss of the larger audience reached by *Daisy Miller* and the novels of Howells; then, the judgment that country-house week ends and the 'season' in London had already provided saturation; then, the shift, in compositional method, from writing to dictation; then, the impetus of admiration from sympathetic younger writers and the allied, induced, partial participation in the new literary movement of the nineties, the 'aesthetic' movement associated with the names of Pater, Wilde, Harland, the *Yellow Book,* and—by extension—of Stevenson, Conrad, Crane, Ford Madox Ford; then, the just completed period of writing for the theater, which produced not only *Guy Domville* but also a conception of the novel as drama; last, the influence, through Maeterlinck and, especially, the later Ibsen, of *symbolisme,* and the return thereby to Hawthorne and a deeper psychology.

The retirement to Rye, which occurred in 1897 when James was fifty-four, distinguished between his life of experience and his life from "past accumulations" (as he once called it). His peregrinations over, he set himself, masterwise, to producing a world compact of all that he had been able, coherently, to think and feel.

Then the process of dictation, beginning with *The Spoils of Poynton,* had its psychological and stylistic consequences. A timid, slow-speaking, stammering boy, Henry had rarely been able to make himself heard at the parental breakfast table. Dictation offered dictatorship: his own voice, uninterrupted by those of more rapid speakers, enabled him to have his oral say in a style which is nearer to his father's than to William's, but slower than his father's. Henry's later manner is an allegro slowed down to a largo, the conversational in apotheosis. 'Literary' as, all sprinkled with its commas of parenthesis, it looks on paper, it is an oral style; and, verifiably, it becomes clear, almost luminous, if recommitted to the voice.

This oral tone was certainly abetted by James's steady turn toward the drama. Rather early, Henry wrote his brother of having mastered the dramatic technique of those makers of the 'well-made play,' Augier and Sardou. He was, of course, an admirer of the Comédie Française and so, we may think, of Molière and Racine. To the French classical drama, as well as to Sardou, I should attribute his increasing use, in his later work, of structure fairly to be called neoclassical, geometrical: wing matching wing, and pilaster corresponding to pilaster, in designs sometimes monstrous in their regularity.

The drama of the nineties, Maeterlinck and, especially, Ibsen, had its effect on the later novels in which, though the author proudly renounces his right of omniscience, he returns triumphantly in the mode of tonality, figuration, almost color scheme. The relation between Kate and Milly, in *The Wings of the Dove,* becomes, at one point, the "likeness of some dim scene in a Maeterlinck play; we have positively the image,

[143]

in the delicate dusk, of the figures so associated and yet so opposed, so mutually watchful: that of the angular pale princess, ostrich-plumed, black-robed—hung about with amulets, reminders, relics—mainly seated, mainly still; and that of the upright, restless, slow-circling lady of her court who exchanges with her, across the black water streaked with evening gleams, fitful questions and answers." There is no question of wholesale admiration. It is the slightly comic because immensely refined and 'cultured' Mrs. Susan Shepherd Stringham who 'admires' Maeterlinck and Pater; but James respected both and in the former could find warrant for a kind of symbolist drama restricted in characters and in action and unified by tone. Ibsen, whose *Hedda* and *Master Builder* he saw, about whom he wrote (in 1891 and 1893) with regard and discernment, gave him examples of fictional work which were the reverse of improvization. "Wrought with admirable closeness is the whole tissue of relations between the five people whom [in *Hedda*] the author sets in motion and on whose behalf he asks of us so few concessions." "The distinguished thing is the firm hand that weaves the web, the deep and ingenious use made of the material." The more one looks at an Ibsen play, the "more intentions" one sees. There was, in the history of the novel, no precedent so near as Ibsen for the concentration of construction and the symbolism which are characteristic of James in the later novels. The patterns of the two have a general parallel of early romanticism, middle realism, and a late maturity which attempts to create what James attributes to the *Master Builder* —a "mingled reality and symbolism."

In poetic drama—*The Tempest* (on which he wrote an essay), the plays of Racine, Maeterlinck, and Ibsen—James came nearest to finding precedents for his later novels. And in these plays are adumbrated the two devices which dominate one's recollection of the later James: close conversation and the metaphor.

Prefacing *The Wings of the Dove*, James differentiated the "picture" from the "drama" as two rival techniques of the novel, a distinction corresponding (I take it) to that between narrative from a 'point of view' and direct presentation. After his experiment, in *The Awkward Age*, with the novel as a set of scenes or dialogues uninterrupted by a unifying consciousness, he grew technically aware, and systematically provident, of dialogue in alternation with narrative, a narrative of consciousness and inner soliloquy.

This technical or structural distinction has its epistemological and metaphysical counterpart. James distinguished two modes of knowing: I shall call them dialectic and myth.

One is a cerebral process, pursued by two or more minds, in contrapuntal movement of thesis, antithesis, synthesis. The topic is attacked from without; the speakers circle around it. Like collaborating detectives they piece together their evidence, or like attorneys for the defense and the prosecution they proceed alternately, on rival systems. There are examinations and cross-examinations. There are mutual misunderstandings, false clues, shifts of position.

James liked to read the reports of divorce trials and murders; he was a confessed admirer of Roughead's books. But it is unnecessary to suppose any external incitation to such close, minute, unwearying analysis as James's people carry on. There are people who find a great dinner or ball or simpler occasion quite unsatisfactory unless before, and especially after, the event there is, in collaboration with another critical observer, an exhaustive analysis of the occasion—its persons, the shifts of relation between them, the discovery of unexpected relations, the probable motives of those present, the intent of speeches and interlocutions which baffled immediacy. James was obviously such a person in his talks with Howard Sturgis, A. C. Benson, Edith Wharton, or Paul Bourget.

By the closeness and intensity of the 'dialectic' James commits himself: he really believes in the all but supreme importance of personal relationships; and, because they are so important, the proper interpretation of them becomes important. Yet relationships between civilized (deep and subtle) people involve concealments as well as avowals; the more developed, the more affectionally, socially, ethically complicated the people, the more precarious and elaborate their relations, and the more imperative the need of system and persistence in making them out.

Unlike the Socratic dialogues, these progress without the aid of a master-mind to control. Nor are they the dialogues of Racine, though in them we come near to James: Miss Gostrey, Mrs. Assingham, Mrs. Stringham are *ficelles,* are confidants, like Phèdre's nurse, Hippolyte's tutor, and Oreste's friend Pylade. But the characteristic dialogue in Racine pits a passionate protagonist against a professional moderator; we might call it the struggle of judgment against passion. In James's, however, the interlocutors are jointly concerned to understand a situation; their passion goes into their seeing. And the confidants do not merely serve to transform soliloquies into dialogues or to draw out their principals; they confer with one another and with other principals. Mrs. Stringham, for example, serves as 'muse' and palace guard and tutor in the 'higher and finer things,' yet she is also a mind intent and alert for conference with Mrs. Lowder and Densher.

The characteristic dialogue of the later novels avoids the long speech—turns, indeed, almost to stichomythia. Even the short speeches are interrupted; and so close is the texture that words and phrases are taken up and returned. Sometimes a figure started by one is developed in turn, after the fashion of *bouts-rimés*. In *The Ivory Tower,* Gray and Horton so collaborate for four pages, as Horton tries to make his friend see the chances to marry, the amorous assailments, which await a rich young American.

The dialogues exhibit the conscious mind working hard and critically scrutinizing all available facts, examining semantically the import of words. This work of intelligence is for James a social act. There is much about ourselves and others which can be got at only in this way; there is a reality which is social, without participation in which we lose our sanity. James seems classical, French, in his whole attitude toward society, intelligence, communication. Unlike Hawthorne's, his people are not tempted by pride to isolate themselves from their fellows; even the shy protagonists are free from pride or inferiority: they reach out their hands to association.

But then there is another kind of truth to be arrived at not socially, intellectually, or analytically but personally, intuitively, imaginatively—through images and symbols. Origins and ends have to be put mythically, as Plato puts them in the *Phaedrus,* the *Gorgias,* the *Republic.* Our reasonings start from an intuition, a total feeling of the nature of the world or the nature of a person; they return constantly to check themselves by that intuition; and it is an intuition upon which, finally, we act. The Jamesian equivalent of myth lies, I think, in the metaphors which, much increasing in *The Wings* over *The Ambassadors,* reach their high richness in *The Bowl* and *The Ivory Tower.*[1]

Here we must distinguish two modes of figuration in the later James. The first is the 'extended conceit' made by prolonging an image, commonly an image proverbial, trite, conventionally 'beautiful.' Instances are frequent in novels; in revising the texture of his earlier work for the New York Edition, James became aware of buried metaphors and resurrected them. Of the following sequence, from *The American* (written in 1877, revised thirty years later), the italicized prelude, anticipating the "sacred fire," was added in 1907: Mrs. Tristram is *"interesting from this sense she gave of her looking for her ideals by a lamp of strange and fitful flame.* She was full—both for good and ill—of beginnings that came to nothing; but she had nevertheless, morally, a spark of the sacred fire." These regalvanized figures, a kind of wit-work, suggest minor 'metaphysical' poetry—that of Henry King or Joseph Beaumont.

The second mode is an emblematic perception, a symbolized intuition—in form an original image, sometimes

1. The three completed masterpieces, *The Ambassadors, The Wings of a Dove,* and *The Golden Bowl,* were written between 1900 and 1904. The order in which these novels were published does not match that of their production: a letter written to Howells in August, 1901, makes clear that *The Ambassadors,* though published a year after *The Wings,* was composed before it; and this discrepancy explains why *The Wings* is in style nearer to *The Bowl.*

Nearly ten years elapsed, years occupied by *The American Scene,* the autobiographical volumes, the revision of the earlier novels, and a return to the writing of plays. Finally, in 1914, when he was seventy, James returned to the novel, first to *The Ivory Tower,* and then, when the war made a contemporary subject unmanageable, to *The Sense of the Past,* a manuscript begun at the period of *The Wings.*

comic, sometimes horrendous, often grotesque. It is these which offer the mythic. The 'expressionism' of the later novels makes it difficult to locate, psychologically, all these emblematic perceptions. Some of James's people—his favorite heroines, certainly—are repeatedly asserted to "image" a situation, that is, instinctly to conceive of it in metaphorical terms. But there is perhaps no character—even to Colonel Assingham—who is not occasionally given a metaphor; and I conclude that James thinks of all his characters as having an unconscious, as having a world of instinctive, feeling reactions, reactions which in art must express themselves (even if by intermediation of the novelist) in metaphoric terms.

Recollected images become metaphors. For years James had traveled diligently in France and Italy, written conscientious commentaries on cathedrals, châteaux, and galleries. Now people remind him of art, become indeed works of art. His heroines, almost without exception, are thus translated. The auburn-haired Milly Theale is a Bronzino; Aurora Coyne becomes "an Italian princess of the *cinque cento:* Titian or the grand Veronese might .... have signed her image." Nan, the modernist and un-British daughter of *The Sense of the Past,* recalls "some mothering Virgin by Van Eyck or Memling." For Maggie there is evoked some slim draped statue from the Vatican, "the smoothed elegant nameless head, the impersonal flit of a creature lost in an alien age." Mme de Vionnet's head could be found on "an old precious medal, some silver coin of the Renaissance," while her daughter is a "faint pastel in an oval frame .... the portrait of an old-time princess." Some embarrassment prevents similar translation of the heroes into paintings or statues; but the Prince (who

[149]

is bought, after all, as a work of art and appraised by his father-in-law with the same taste which appraises a Luini) can scarcely be described except out of art history: by way of representing the superior utility and weight of the male, James renders him in architecture. His eyes, for example, prompt the *concetto* of their being "the high windows of a Roman palace, of an historic front by one of the great old designers, thrown open on a feast day to the golden air." And his union to the Ververs, the new 'relation' which it establishes, suggests to Adam Verver that "their decent little old-time union, Maggie's and his own, had resembled a good deal some pleasant public square, in the heart of an old city, into which a great Palladian church, say—something with a grand architectural front,—had suddenly been dropped."

The obvious errand of these analogies is honorific; they belong to the high and hallowed world of 'culture.' But in the decorative and the 'beautiful,' James's taste (like his taste in poetry) was conventional. He had to come to the poetic by misapprehension, one might say, by the way of the unlovely.

Unlike his Prince, who "never saw .... below a certain social plane," James had looked observantly, in his days of "notation," at zoos and aquariums and circuses; and he remembered the crowded perceptions of "A Small Boy" in a remote America. Having neither children nor wealth, Mrs. Assingham confronted "two great holes to fill, and she described herself as dropping social scraps into them as she had known old ladies, in her early, American time, drop morsels of silk into baskets in which they collected the material for some eventual patchwork quilt." For regression to the 'good old,' there are the childhood images: Adam Verver, indulging a tiny holiday from responsibility, seems "caught in the act of handling a relic of infancy,—sticking on the head of a broken soldier or trying the lock of a wooden gun." In their continued intimacy after both have other mates, father and daughter were "at times, the dear things, like children playing at visits, playing at 'Mr. Thompson and Mrs. Fane.'"

The chief occasions for 'imaging' are perceptions of persons and personal relations. In *The Bowl* and the unfinished novels, the characters are not visualized analytically but felt for us, rendered in terms of the total impression they make. Book I of *The Ivory Tower* is constantly metaphorical, moving into dialectical prose only to chronicle the Bradhams' large, busy tea. Rosanna, her father, the Bradhams, and Cissy Foy, their protégée, appear in poetry. Rosanna's massiveness and heroic stature and indomitability are rendered by the recurrent image of the ship in full sail; her voice rings out like that of Brünnehilde at the opera; her parasol is the "roof of some Burmese palanquin or perhaps even pagoda"; her presence is apprehended by Cissy as that of "some seated idol, a great Buddha perched upon a shrine."[2] Though he owns the literal stage property of a rocking chair on a vacant Newport piazza, Rosanna's father is also "a ruffled hawk, motionless but for his single tremor"; he broods "after the fashion of a philosopher tangled in some maze of metaphysics." When he makes his single shift of gear, from business to his daughter, he passes from his "market" into "some large cool dusky temple, a place where idols others than those of his worship vaguely loomed and gleamed."

2. James's oriental figures are relatively frequent and always to be attended; they habitually betoken the strangeness of that East which is East and hence incommunicable to the West.

The zealous exegete of meanings studies his companions' faces. He sees that Verver's face "resembled a small decent room, clean-swept and unencumbered with furniture, but drawing special advantages .... from the outlook of a pair of ample and uncurtained windows"; that Davy Bradham's "good worn worldly face, superficially so smooth," had "the sense of it lined and scratched and hacked across much in the manner of the hard ice of a large pond at the end of a long day's skating." Densher notes it "an oddity of Mrs. Lowder's that her face in speech was like a lighted window at night, but that silence immediately drew the curtain."

Our recollection of Mrs. Lowder, James's massive rich British matron, is almost entirely compounded from the imagings of Densher, through whose at once admiring and hostile and amused consciousness we chiefly see her. The master metaphor is metallic. We first view her in her cage— all "perpetual satin, twinkling bugles and flashing gems, with a lustre of agate eyes, a sheen of raven hair, a polish of complexion," encased in the hard glittering surface of armor. Later, at the dinner table, managing a conversation, she becomes a steamboat, "steering a course in which she called at subjects as if they were islands in an archipelago," resumes, "with a splash of the screw, her cruise among the islands." Still later she has "something in common, even in repose, with a projectile, of great size, loaded and ready for use."

Mrs. Midmore, briefly presented in *The Sense of the Past,* and Mrs. Newsome, indirectly presented, never seen, belong, by their analogical treatment, to the same category with Mrs. Lowder: they are women as massive as, ultimately, menacing. It is never entirely clear how far Strether understands his feeling toward Mrs. Newsome (or how completely James understands it): Mrs. Newsome is not, like Mrs. Lowder, an obvious case of Philistinism; indeed, regards herself as an apostle of Culture—of the higher and finer and rarer and newer thought; and James apparently wants to represent Strether as making a sacrifice in renouncing Mrs. Newsome (as well as the more suitable Miss Gostrey). Yet, though the Lady of Woolett represented maternal protection as well as maternal domination, Strether's chief sense, upon losing her, must, like Lewes' upon losing the great Eliot, have been relief.[3] Mrs. Newsome is massive because she has no imagination. She rests, sits, *is*—a fact without resilience. Others, the imaginative, must adjust, accommodate. As he thinks of her, Strether's "eyes might have been fixing some particularly large iceberg in a cool blue northern sea."

If Philistines are to be "imaged" as inflexibly massive, metallic (unimaginative), the children of light owe their erect posture, their equilibrium, to their flexibility. They summon up recollection of ballet dancers, show people, brave ritualists who perform, upon exhibition, feats of persistence and agility: figures proper to Goya, Degas, Toulouse-Lautrec. Assingham watches his wife engaged at her favorite social analysis "much as he had sometimes watched at the Aquarium the celebrated lady who, in a slight, though tight, bathing suit, turned somersaults or did tricks in the tank of water which looked so cold and uncomfortable to the non-amphibious." When Maggie, courageously, undertakes a grand dinner at Portland Place, Mrs. Assingham assists "like one of the assistants in the ring at the circus, to keep up the pace of the sleek revolving animal on whose back the lady in short spangled skirts should

3. I am remembering an anecdote told by Stephen Spender in *The Destructive Element,* one of the best studies of James.

brilliantly caper and posture." Throughout most of her half of *The Golden Bowl,* Maggie is the "overworked little trapezist girl." The novel rehearses her progress from being a child to being the lady in spangled skirts who can keep her balance while she capers on the back of a horse.

There are other fresh aspects of Maggie to be celebrated— for one, her resourceful Americanism—in contrast to her husband's ancient, aristocratic lineage. By virtue of this difference, Maggie must be expected to do most of the 'adjustment': she must act like a "settler or trader in a new country; in the likeness even of some Indian squaw with a papoose on her back and barbarous bead work to sell." But without question there are governing images. As Maggie is the trapezist, so Charlotte, through the corresponding second half of *The Bowl,* is some wild creature, tormented by the gadfly; she is a caged creature which, bending the gilt bars, has escaped to roam; she wears "a long silken halter looped round her beautiful neck."

In the later novels the chief thing, after all, is the structure. The characters exist in relations, and we are unbidden to information about them irrelevant to the fable and the relations. A character might almost be defined as the locus at which a given number of relations join. The Prince, for example, is the total of his relations to Mrs. Assingham, Mr. Verver, Charlotte, and Maggie: though he has to be preliminarily posited as a classic instance of the aristocratic European, James presents that datum as summarily as possible.

One who, like Gray Fielder and his creator, is "critico-analytically interested" in people, gives inevitable attention to defining relationships. His skilled attention delights in the idea of a little set or group (like Mrs. Brook's), capable of developing its own vocabulary of allusions and words; but he specializes on the relation between two. Hawthorne was James's great predecessor in this study, especially in those masterly chapters of *The Scarlet Letter* describing Chillingworth's sadistic operations on Dimmesdale. Relationships are not static and are never so represented by James; and the change in one relationship affects a corresponding change in another. 'Critico-analytical' people do not take fixity of relationship for granted but are constantly attempting to name the new state into which a relationship has entered, the new quality which has emerged. The relations most "imaged" are likely to be those which can least be talked out. Maria Gostrey and Strether do not "image" one another because the relation between them is dialectical; but, since Chad (for all his wonderful renovation) is neither dialectical nor imaginative, Strether has strenuously to use his own intuitive instrument. When Strether first encounters the Paris Version, Chad's "attitude was that of a person who has been gracefully quiet while the messenger at last reaching him has run a mile through the dust." And much later, Strether perceives that Chad 'puts out' his excitement or whatever emotion "as he put out his washing...... It was quite for Strether himself in short to feel a personal analogy with the laundress bringing home the triumphs of the mangle."

The relation between Merton Densher and Kate Croy, particularly, rewards study, for Densher at least (whom we see more from within than we see Kate) is not only dialectically clever but also passionate. We wonder how he can tolerate Kate's plan or Kate for her plan; but, granting that his conscious mind found it "something so extraordinarily special to Kate that he felt himself shrink from the complications in-

[155]

volved in judging it," we discover him, nonetheless, transcending his complicity. He is drawn to her by desire yet repelled as well as fascinated by her calculations. As he looks at her, in the Gallery, the sight plays on his pride of possession, "as a hidden master in a great dim church might play on the grandest organ"; yet this sense of possession is more than matched by apprehension of her calculating power: more than once he said to her, "You keep the key of the cupboard, and I foresee that when we're married you'll dole me out my sugar by lumps."

In *The Sense of the Past,* the most "imaged" relation is between Ralph Pendrel, American introspective, and the blunt, massive, extroverted Perry Midmore, his contrary. When the other Regency and British Midmores are puzzled by the visitor, Perry has the advantage of not being 'cultured': he trusts, animal-like, to his instincts, scents the presence of the clever and alien "as some creature of the woods might scent the bait of the trapper ...."; "like a frightened horse," he "sniffs in the air the nearness of some creature of a sort he has never seen." It is Perry, in turn, who most makes Ralph aware of his general peril, the precariousness of sustaining his role—how he must always use *manner* as a weapon, always "work from *behind* something—something that, look as it would, he must object to Perry's staring at in return as if it were a counterfeit coin or a card from up his sleeve."

The most powerful, most inclusive, vision in this novel sums Ralph's sudden awareness of his 1820 Midmores in their historic, their psychic, distance from him. In a somewhat similar moment of perception, Alice saw her companions as nothing but playing cards. Ralph sees his as waxworks or statues: "an artful, a wonderful trio, some mechanic but consummate imitation of ancient life, staring through the vast plate of a museum." This perception marks the turn from Ralph's desire to live in the past to his countermovement: James's hero, who disappoints his robust lady by his passionate love of the past, his desire to catch "the very tick of the old stopped clocks," is cured of his wish by its fulfilment and at the end returns, happily, to the modern world.

The second half of *The Golden Bowl,* supreme among the later novels for the density and richness of its symbolism, is dominated by Maggie's sense of the relations in which she stands, of which the most stable is with her father, the most precarious and menacing that with her rival, the Dark Lady.

The "imagings"—fear-images, many of them—which crowd the later chapters arise from Maggie's inability to talk out her apprehensions except, and scantily, to Mrs. Assingham. Her relations to her father, the Prince, and Charlotte cannot, by the very nature of her problem and her project, be socially articulated; she must fight soundlessly and in the dark.

When the "little trapezist girl" tries to envisage her plight she often does so in architectural mode. The strangeness which she suddenly stumbles over—Charlotte's affair with the Prince—is an "outlandish pagoda, a structure plated with bright porcelain, colored and figured and adorned at the overhanging eaves with silver bells that tinkled," a pagoda set down in her own familiar, blooming garden. Later, in Book V, she feels the whole horrible situation to constitute the central chamber of a haunted house, "a great overarched and overglazed rotunda where gaiety might reign, but the doors of which opened into sinister circular passages." What Maggie must take in is the possibility of an evil which can appear in a Garden, or in a Home—which is not the villain of a melodrama or the Devil replete with horns. Evil met her, now, "like some bad-faced stranger surprised in one of the thick-carpeted corridors of a house of quiet on a Sunday afternoon." The sense of imprisonment is impossible to avoid, even when it is an enclosure allegedly therapeutic. Shut off from responsibility by the social gifts of her husband and his mistress, Maggie, coming to, finds herself locked up "in the solid chamber of her helplessness as in a bath of benevolence artfully prepared for her..... Baths of benevolence were all very well, but at least, unless one was a patient of some sort, a nervous eccentric or a lost child, one usually wasn't so immersed save by one's own request."

These oppressive claustric figures give way, as Maggie turns active, to more agile figures. In Book V, Maggie, feeling like a scapegoat, goes off into the darkness. From the terrace, looking in through the window, she sees her companions glassed, separated off like actors on a stage. Equipped with this perspective, she begins to fight; and even though images of frustration continue, they are intermitted with those of triumph. She overcomes her fear of Charlotte, lies boldly, kisses her with magnanimous treachery, and begins to "image" Charlotte's defeat; psychically hears, issuing from beneath her elegant mask, the "shriek of a soul in pain." Now out of prison, Maggie sees her companions caught: her husband strikes her as being "caged" in his room; and our final view of Charlotte, consigned for shipment to American City, is that of a once living creature now petrified into "some colored and gilded image."

There are *données* of *The Bowl* which are perverse and scarcely to be accepted. Since James cannot really bring himself to 'realize' a union at once sexual and 'good,' the loves of the book are the passion of Charlotte for the Prince and of Maggie for her father. Dialectic, managed by another than James, might usefully have made these presuppositions explicit. But, to the saving of the novel's balance, the violent relation is between two women; and, whatever the pretext or the booty, Maggie becames aware that evil may meet one garbed as an urbane friend and learns how so to fight evil as to save what she prizes. James's sense of the good is, one might say, temperamentally conditioned; his sense of evil is normal and sound. And the great theme of *The Bowl* is the discovery that evil exists in the forms most disruptive to civilization: in disloyalty and treason.

In spite of the predominance of myth over dialectic in the novel, especially its second half, *The Bowl* does not represent James's escape into a defeatist Unconscious, the collapse of his system of values. Unlike many of his protagonists, Maggie is concerned not only to understand her situation but to will, savingly, and to act, successfully. Her dreams are, ultimately, those not of a patient but of a victor.

The tension in James between the dialectic and the mythic is an epistemological way of naming that rich interplay and reconciliation of impulses which constitutes his great achievement. As a person and as a writer, he matured slowly; he had to confront the long, slow business of synthesizing his impulse to merge and his impulse to withdraw, his shyness and his sociability, his romanticism (his first literary mode) and his realism, his humanism and his mysticism.

If there is the Henry James who speaks of dining out a hundred and seven times in a winter, who is to be "imaged" in the ritual garments—the silk topper, the morning coat, the fawn-colored waistcoat, the gloves folded in hand—there is also the inner James who never leaves the sanctuary, where are the altars of literature, the dead, and the Good.

One must not talk here, of appearance and reality, for that is not the relation between this pair. In terms from the characterology (or perhaps hagiography) of James's youth, one can say that the outer self was modeled on Norton or Russell Lowell, while the inner self remained not remote from Emerson—if one may add, from Hawthorne, what James found deficient in Emerson, a "sense of the dark, the foul, the base .... certain complications in life .... human perversity." The outer James is an urbane humanist, an intelligent, if precise, defender of convention, usage, social discrimination, and social intelligence; the inner James is an intuitionist, possessed of a deep nonutilitarian, nontraditional faith in goodness for goodness' sake, loyalty to loyalty, *caritas*.

Because James was a 'thinker' only on the theory of fiction, he did not schematize, still less adjust, his levels. He reported honestly whatever—material, social, spiritual—he saw. He liked breeding, culture, taste; he perceived that these were the products (even if not the necessary products) of leisure, and leisure, in turn, of money. Yet from youth to age he gave unpleasant pictures of the merely intelligent and cultivated— of the elder Bellegardes, of Osmond and Mme Merle, of Mrs. Gereth, Mrs. Newsome, Mrs. Brookenham. They are all "wonderful" specimens—expensive to produce and engaging to study; but they do not give us our scale. High above the bright and cultivated are the good.

To be sure, he finds it difficult to work out his sum. His 'good people' are generally poor, like Fleda Vetch and Strether; when, like Milly Theale and the Ververs, they are rich, it is by fabulous endowment: Adam's alleged power of making money remains unconvincing. By the time he wrote *The Ivory Tower,* James seems to have agreed with the Gospels that the salvation of the rich is precarious. Yet he as clearly believed that salvation—or total salvation—was, in any case, rare. If riches could prevent it, so could envy, brutality, and stupidity, the vices of the poor, or the complacence of 'middle-class morality.'

This range of standards in James makes him both rewarding and exacting. His irony, which is pervasive, can be most readily detected in his act of praising people for having a virtue or two, virtues on which they plume themselves, when his criterion is a stratified perfection.

The danger of such a philosophy is that, in its awareness, its inclusiveness, it shall turn finally skeptical, or regard uncertainty and complexity as final virtues. This seems, in practice, not to have happened to James: though he probably had his confusions and timidities, he was not awarely proud of them. The general view of him, until fifteen years ago, scaled him down to a caricatured 'humanism,' that is, to snobbery and Anglophilism—though better evidence can be collected for his disapproval of 'high society,' for his Americanism and his moralism. He was emphatically not a skeptic or a believer in mutual cancellations. He had a clear hierarchy of values, or, better, a hierarchy of value-series, which he applied with almost equal realism and rigor.

The distinctive, masterly achievement of Henry James in his maturity is a series of 'metaphysical' novels in which, working as a poet, he incarnates the interrelations between the conscious and the unconscious, between the social and the subjective.

1943

INDEX OF NAMES

INDEX

Pascal, Blaise, 79
Pater, Walter, 54, 67, 75, 101, 102, 144
Patmore, Coventry, 62
Péguy, Charles, 68
Péladan, Sar, 74
Phillips, Ambrose, 41, 42
Pierce, Franklin, 87
Piers Plowman, 60
Plato, 38, 110, 131, 147
Plotinus, 80
Poe, Edgar Allan, 43, 140
Pope, Alexander, 136
Pound, Ezra, 59
Powys, T. F., 124
Prior, Matthew, 40
Proust, Marcel, 48, 102, 122
Psichari, Ernest, 68

Quarles, Francis, 2, 3, 8, 12, 29

Racine, Jean, 143, 146
Radcliffe, Ann, 93, 94, 96
Reynolds, Sir Joshua, 54
Roughead, William, 145
Ruskin, John, 19, 54–55
Russell, George (A.E.), 67, 78, 79, 82, 83

St. John, 12
St. John of the Cross, 117
St. Teresa, 117
Santayana, George, 123, 129
Sardou, Victorien, 143
Scott, Sir Walter, 85, 96, 99
Selden, John, 26
Sennett, Mack, 106
Shaftesbury, Third Earl of, 136
Shakespeare, William, 144
Shelley, P. B., 67
Shenstone, William, 40
Sheridan, Richard Brinsley, 47
Sinnett, A. P., 71
Smart, Christopher, 40

Sophocles, 128, 130
Spender, Stephen, 118, 153
Spenser, Edmund, 40, 48, 92
Sturgis, Howard, 146
Summers, Montague, 94
Swedenborg, Emanuel, 67, 74, 77–78
Swift, Jonathan, 81, 112
Sylvester, Joshua, 3

Taylor, Jeremy, 9
Thomas of Celano, 32
Thoreau, Henry David, 70
Titian, 149
Tolstoi, L. N., 84
Tompson, Benjamin, 6
Toulouse-Lautrec, 153
Traherne, Thomas, 35
Trench, Richard C., 61
Trollope, Anthony, 23, 86
Tynan, Katherine, 68

Van Eyck, Jan, 149
Vaughan Henry, 35
Verlaine, Paul, 69
Veronese, Paul, 149
Villon, François, 83
Virgil, 37, 38, 49

Waller, Edmund, 38
Walton, Izaak, 20
Warlock, Peter, 64
Warton, Joseph, 41, 42
Wells, Henry W., 59
Wendell, Barrett, 95
Wharton, Edith, 146
Whipple, E. P., 86
White, Alison G., vii
Whitman, Walt, 9, 83
Williams, Vaughan, 64
Woolf, Virginia, 120
Wordsworth, William, 48
Wren, Christopher, 20

Young, Edward, 38

SELECTED ANN ARBOR PAPERBACKS

works of enduring merit

For a complete list of Ann Arbor Paperback titles write:
THE UNIVERSITY OF MICHIGAN PRESS / ANN ARBOR